TELLING GOD'S STORY

TELLING GOD'S STORY

National Mission Congress 2000

Resources and Documents

EPISCOPAL COMMISSION ON MISSION

Catholic Bishops' Conference of the Philippines

James H. Kroeger, M.M.
General Editor

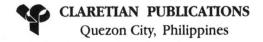

CLARETIAN PUBLICATIONS
Quezon City, Philippines

TELLING GOD'S STORY: National Mission Congress 2000
Resources and Documents

Copyright @ 2001 by:

Catholic Bishops'Conference of the Philippines
470 General Luna Street, Intramuros, Manila.
Tels: 527-4054 • 527-4138 • FAX: 527-4063
E-mail: cbcp@info.com.ph • Website: www.cbcp.net

Published 2001 by:

Claretian Publications, Inc.
U.P.P.O. Box 4 Diliman, 1101 Quezon City, Philippines
Tel.: 921-3984 • FAX: 921-7429
E-mail: claret@cnl.net   Website: www.cnl.net/claret

Claretian Publications is a pastoral endeavor of the Claretian Missionaries in the Philippines. It aims to promote a renewed spirituality rooted in the process of total liberation and solidarity in response to the needs, challenges, and pastoral demands of the Church today.

Professional Services: A. Dy, F. Alvarez, P. Dy
Front cover photograph: J. Kroeger
Back cover painting: B. Justiniano

Library of Congress Cataloging-in-Publication Data

Catholic Bishops'Conference of the Philippines
Kroeger, James H., 1945- (General Editor)
TELLING GOD'S STORY
National Mission Congress 2000
Resources and Documents
p. viii + 140 cm. 15.24 x 22.86
ISBN 971-501-891-2

1. Missions—Theory. 2. Missions—Catechesis.
3. Missions—Philippines. 4. Catholic Church—Missions.
5. Catholic Church—Congresses—Philippines. I. Title.
II. Catholic Bishops'Conference of the Philippines.
III. Kroeger, J. (James)

BV2090.T45a   2001
266—dc20a   CIP

CONTENTS

Preface vii

I. CONGRESS OVERVIEWS 1

    Mission Congress 2000 (Manuel) 3

    Celebrating a Congress (Arévalo) 13

II. INTRODUCTIONS 19

III. CONGRESS PICTORIAL 31

IV. ADDRESSES AND PRESENTATIONS 41

    Mission Theology (Tagle) 43

    Proclamation (Gomez) 51

    Inculturation (Estepa) 59

    Interreligious Dialogue (McCahill) 67

    Theology of Dialogue (Kroeger) 75

    Human Promotion (Hechanova) 81

    Paschal Spirituality (Huang) 91

V. HOMILIES AND REFLECTIONS 97

VI. OFFICIAL DOCUMENTS 107

    Mission Congress Message 109

    CBCP Pastoral Letter on Mission 115

VII. ADDITIONAL RESOURCES 125

    FABC and Mission (Malone) 127

    Art and Mission (Kroeger) 133

PREFACE

Mission means "Telling God's Story." To be in mission signifies that, at heart, one has heard the Good News, reflected deeply on its crucial importance, integrated the message into one's life, and then passionately desires to tell others, to "tell the world of His love," to tell God's love story, that love made incarnate, the Jesus-story. Missioners and evangelizers alike will testify that this story is, from beginning to end, a story of great compassion and mercy, a salvation story.

"Cebu 2000," as the National Mission Congress is sometimes called, was an event centered on stories of deep faith. The Philippine bishops, men and women religious, laity, visitors, youth and adults, who came to Cebu were deeply inspired by the presentations, liturgies, celebrations, and experiences of the congress. "Cebu 2000" became its own story—the story of a local Church dedicated to mission and evangelization at the turn of a new millennium. "Cebu 2000" was a central event in the Jubilee Story of the Philippine Church.

Story-telling in faith was the integrating methodology of the mission congress. In more academic language it could be termed "narrative missiology." By all accounts this methodology proved successful: it communicated, it inspired, it brought laughter, it engendered joyful enthusiasm, it strengthened faith, it elicited commitment. God's love story and concrete mission experience became interwoven with the participants' own story of faith, love, and committed service.

This slim volume, *Telling God's Story,* presents the highlights of "Cebu 2000." Here one finds congress overviews, messages, formal presentations, homilies, reflections, and Church documents. All are meant to communicate the "Cebu Story," the speakings of the Spirit during those five inspiring days.

Readers will quickly observe that the entire congress story is not presented here (a full record of the Congress *Acta* is planned by the CBCP Commission on Mission). This volume contains selections, highlights, and pivotal insights drawn from the entire proceedings: congress messages, homilies and reflections are treated briefly; major addresses are usually complete; workshop statements and recommendations await another volume; official documents are found in their entirety; photographs help tell the "Cebu Story."

Telling God's Story, therefore, is no more than a brief, popular presentation of the rich, moving, grace-filled, Spirit-inspired First National Mission Congress. Finally, entrusting all to God's loving providence and the Spirit's inspiration, it is sincerely hoped and desired that "Cebu 2000" will result in a new generation of missioners—women and men, religious and lay, especially the youth—who will emerge from the Philippine Church to go and "Tell the World of His Love," to tell God's Love Story in this new millennium.

Epiphany 2001   Editor

Part One

CONGRESS

OVERVIEWS

THE NATIONAL MISSION CONGRESS 2000

Vicente C. Manuel, SVD

INTRODUCTION

D uring the 78th Bishops' Plenary Assembly held on January 27-29, 1999, the Catholic Bishops' Conference of the Philippines (CBCP) unanimously decided to hold a National Mission Congress (NMC).

On February 2, 1999, Archbishop Oscar Cruz, CBCP President, wrote to inform the Congregation for the Evangelization of Peoples (CEP) of the Philippine Bishops' decision and to seek the approval for the National Mission Congress. In his letter he said, "it is our most fitting culminating activity to end our triennium of preparation for the Great Jubilee Year—*fully aware of our commitment to mission in Asia and the rest of the world.*"

His Eminence Josef Cardinal Tomko, CEP Cardinal Prefect, answered on March 1, 1999. He wrote, "While welcoming and approving this initiative, we hope and pray that, as the new Millennium approaches, such a national event will renew and strengthen the Church in the Philippines in her evangelizing mission."

By the middle of March 1999, the date and venue of the congress were decided. His Eminence Ricardo Cardinal Vidal graciously accepted to host the

National Mission Congress in the Archdiocese of Cebu, the birthplace of Christianity in the Philippines. The date for the congress was from September 27 to October 1, 2000; it would include two important feasts: San Lorenzo Ruiz (September 28); Saint Therese of the Child Jesus, Patroness of Mission (October 1).

The Bishops determined the tone and direction of the congress: *commitment to mission.* Rome stamped its approval with the wish that the event would renew and strengthen the Philippine Church's evangelizing mission. With the date and venue of the Congress decided, the task of awakening the Philippine Church to its missionary responsibility through a National Mission Congress was at hand.

The Philippine Church has to become a "local-church-in-mission" in spirit and in fact, if it is to meet the expectations of Pope John Paul II and the previous Holy Fathers who, time and again, have expressed the desire that Filipino Catholics be the foremost missionaries in Asia. Moreover, the Second Plenary Council of the Philippines (PCP-II) put the Philippine Church in the state of mission. The National Congress on Mission provides the opportune occasion to discuss how to carry forward and implement more intensely the mission thrust of PCP-II.

PRE-CONGRESS PREPARATIONS

Consultations and Initial Decisions. The Episcopal Commission on Mission, together with the Pontifical Mission Society of the Philippines, helped and guided by theologians and missiologists, held several consultations from February to July 1999. Invited to participate in the consultations were various CBCP Episcopal Commissions, the Association of Major Religious Superiors of Men and Women in the Philippines, the Council of the Laity, Lay Movements, the Office of Women, the Youth, etc. Enthusiasm and interest for the mission congress, willingness and promise of assistance shaped the prevailing sentiment and atmosphere that pervaded the meetings.

Among the first things discussed and clarified were the objectives of the mission congress which were: **first,** to reaffirm and explain to the ordinary Catholic faithful that, *every Christian, without exception, every baptized person, by the sacrament of initiation, is a missionary.* It was hoped that this would reawaken an interest in and a commitment to missionary action in and by Filipino Catholics; **second**, to explain and clarify how the Catholic Church today understands mission emerging from the changes initiated by the Second Vatican Council. This second objective incorporates the shifts in the understanding of mission found in *Evangelii Nuntiandi*, *Redemptoris Missio*, and *Ecclesia in Asia*.

A very important decision was made concerning the methodology, that is, the way of presenting and explaining the different dimensions of mission. The approach was to be through story-telling, through "narratives," by *de facto* missionaries from at home and abroad. They were to narrate how they proclaim Jesus in different life situations, among people of different faiths and cultures, among the destitute and marginalized. They were to share how they proclaim Jesus by their witness of life, by their presence, by listening—through dialogue. In short, it means "re-telling the Jesus Story" as lived and experienced by missionaries.

The decision about story-telling was of no little significance. The methodology (story-telling) of presenting the topics is interesting, simple and understandable, even to lay people. It has a deep and lasting impact. Stories are remembered most, especially personal accounts and life witness of heroism and living the faith. After the story-sharing the participants would be guided to understand more deeply the theological bases of mission and helped find principles for missionary action, through a variety of workshops.

The contemporary teaching of the Church about the different components of integral evangelization, namely, proclamation, inculturation, interreligious dialogue, human promotion, and spirituality composed the main topics of the daily working sessions. Fifteen other individual mission topics were added for workshops: "Re-inventing" Mission; Formation for Mission; Basic Ecclesial Communities; Religious Life and Mission; Laity and Mission; Mission *ad gentes*; Family and Mission; Media and Mission; Women and Mission; Migrants and Mission; Mary, Therese and Mission; Contemplation and Mission; Pontifical Mission Societies; Jesus, Eucharist and Mission; Youth and Mission.

Two-Phase Strategy. With the venue of National Mission Congress in Cebu and the majority of the members of the Executive Committee residing in Manila, a two-phase strategy, namely, Pre-Congress Period and Congress Proper was adopted. The time-frame, the delineated tasks, and an organizational chart were established.

The Pre-Congress Period designates the time from the decision of the Bishops to hold the congress up to the congress proper celebration in Cebu. This period was focused on the task of generating missionary awareness, involvement and commitment of all institutions and levels of the Philippine Church; catechesis, consultations/assemblies and other related activities like mission exhibits, theatrical presentations, mission exposures, prayers-vigils-fasting for missions were recommended. During this phase, the base of activities was the dioceses, parishes, BECs, schools, and other religious institutions like the seminaries, and Church organizations and movements.

The National Mission Congress Proper, on the other hand, consists of the calendar of activities during the national gathering of delegates for the purpose of celebrating the unique missionary role and character of the Philippine Church as part of the Jubilee Year celebrations. The actual celebration (September 27 to October 1, 2000) in Cebu was to emphasize our missionary commitment to Asia and the rest of the world.

The Organigram. The organizational chart of the National Mission Congress is a consequence of the two-phase strategy. A simple description of the organizational chart includes several elements. Under the CBCP and the Honorary Presidents of the National Mission Congress 2000, one finds the National Executive Committee, the over-all organizer of the whole affair. The National Executive Committee has two Secretariats: the National, Manila-based, Secretariat and the Cebu-based Secretariat.

The Manila-based Secretariat coordinates all pre-congress activities, ranging from official communication of information (sent by the National Executive Committee to Bishops and other institutions and groups) to mission awareness campaigns through posters, brochures, and printing of catechetical materials on mission, to promotion and publicity through print, radio and television, to registration of national delegates, etc.; in short, all pre-Congress activities.

The Cebu-based Secretariat, on the other hand, is responsible for the Congress proper; this entails: registration of participants, program implementation (e.g. opening ceremonies), liturgy, documentation, exhibits, physical and technical facilities, workshop sites, accommodations, transportation, speakers, security, etc.

Through a series of regular meetings organized by the National Executive Committee, the plans and program of activities of the two Secretariats were discussed, monitored and coordinated. The strategy proved the Cebu Secretariat truly capable of managing a congress of such magnitude.

General Methodology and Process. The methodology and process of the National Mission Congress was adopted to insure the smooth running of the congress, the attainment of the objectives of the congress, and the satisfaction of the participants. The two thousand three hundred participants—all representatives from every ecclesiastical circumscription, religious congregation of men and women, laity and youth—were divided into two workshop groups.

Those in the specialized groups, numbering 800, were further divided into forty participants each for the twenty specialized workshops. The competent facilitators of these specialized workshops were selected from a cross-section of religious congregations and lay movements; each was given the responsibility to prepare and conduct the workshop. They received guidelines concerning the conduct of the workshops. Each workshop was expected to have a one-page concluding statement as well as some resolutions to be presented in the general assembly. Moreover, the facilitators were to help the participants get a profound understanding of the theme so that they, in turn, could become "trainer-multipliers" on mission when they returned home after the congress. For the organizers of the Mission Congress, the success or the failure of the congress depended largely on productive workshops.

The General Workshops, on the other hand, were constituted by the participants who were not in the Specialized Workshops. They were conducted in four selected Cebu parishes: Our Lady of the Sacred Heart, Capitol Parish; Saint Therese Parish, Lahug; Asilo de la Medalla Milagrosa; and, St. Joseph Parish, Mabolo. The delegates, together with the parishioners of these parishes and possible walk-in visitors from other provinces, received mission catechesis by competent speakers drawn from throughout the Philippines.

The order of the day, except for the opening and closing days, began with morning praise, followed by the plenary session during which the main speakers shared their stories and reflections. The afternoons were for the workshops; each day ended with the Eucharistic Celebration. Except for the opening day, each day was dedicated in honor of a saint; the last day, October 1, was in honor of Saint Therese, Patroness of Mission.

Special events were included within the schedule, e.g. a tour of Cebu historical sites because for the majority of congress delegates, this was their first time in Cebu. Two distinguished visitors, namely, Archbishop Charles A. Schleck, CSC of the CEP in Rome, and Father Edward Malone, MM of the FABC in Hong Kong, were conferred Honorary Degrees of Doctor of Laws and Doctor of Humanities respectively, by the University of San Carlos under the Divine Word Fathers.

Highlights of the Pre-Congress Period. The Pre-Congress Period contained many highlights; some of the more significant ones are presented:

A: The official launching in the dioceses of the mission congress, however low-key it may have been. This occurred on October 24, 1999. The Bishops were asked to publicize the launching in their respective circumscriptions, start the prayer for the mission congress, have their own mission awareness activities, and request help from the Pontifical Mission Societies for mission animation activities.

B: Support of the National Mission Congress by the Association of Major Religious Superiors of Men and Women in the Philippines. The chairpersons and the Executive Board of the association gave the mission congress their enthusiastic commitment.

C: The Workshop-Seminar of the Bishops on *Ecclesia in Asia*, before the January 2000 General Assembly of the Bishops; it was attended by over sixty bishops. The bishops approved the proposal to establish a Missiological Institute where the dioceses could be updated and our people trained for mission. After the January 2000 CBCP meeting, mission congresses were held in the Bicol Region, Southern Tagalog Region, Northern and Central Luzon Regions, plus in the archdioceses of Manila and Naga and in the dioceses of Malolos, Alaminos, Naga, Sorsogon, Daet, Abra, and Cabanatuan. A complete record of what transpired in the Visayas and Mindanao is unavailable, but surely the dioceses had their own mission activities. Bishop G. Camiña held his own diocesan congress. Archbishop O. Gordoncillo actively promoted the prayer for the mission congress.

D: The preparation of several printed and audio materials for mission catechesis, namely, (1) *Mission Animation Resource Kit (MARK)*, prepared for the Bishops' Workshop-Seminar on Mission before the January 2000 General Assembly; (2) *Tell the World... Catechetical Modules for Mission Animation*, consisting of ten mission modules and designed to help spread enthusiasm and commitment to mission. As catechetical material for mission animation, it is as useful now as before the mission congress. Both *MARK* and *Tell the World...* are edited by James H. Kroeger, MM; (3) *Mission and the Philippines, Past, Present and Future* by Francis X. Clark, SJ; (4) The Theme Song of the Mission Congress *We are Gifts*, composed by Father Carlo Magno S. Marcelo, composer of the *Jubilee Song*. It is available in cassette tapes with seven other mission songs.

E: The CBCP Pastoral Letter on Mission: ***"Missions" and the Church in the Philippines***: *A Pastoral Letter on the Church's Mission in the New Millennium*. For years to come, this letter will be the main reference for the Church of the Philippines in discussions about our obligation to share the faith we have received.

F: The majority of the Bishops leading their diocesan delegates to attend the National Mission Congress in Cebu or sending their delegates for the Congress. There was one hundred percent participation of the dioceses. The Bishops' support for the mission congress has been shown in many other ways.

MISSION CONGRESS PROPER

The National Mission Congress in Cebu was honored by and blessed with the presence of His Eminence John Baptist Cardinal Wu of the Diocese of Hong Kong as Papal Legate. The Congregation for the Evangelization of Peoples was represented by Archbishop Charles A. Schleck, CSC. Philippine Ambassador to the Holy See, Hon. Henrietta de Villa, came from Rome just for the occasion. Archbishop Antonio Franco, Apostolic Nuncio to the Philippines, was present the entire time. Jaime Cardinal L. Sin and former President Corazon C. Aquino graced the occasion. Archbishop Orlando Quevedo, President of the CBCP, led the majority of the Bishops of the Philippines for the celebration. Cardinal Ricardo Vidal of Cebu, with his auxiliary bishops, with the clergy, the laity and individual families opened their hearts and homes to the 2,300 visitor-delegates from all over the Philippines, some coming from Kalayan Island of Batanes, others from Jolo, Sulu, led by their respective bishops.

Filipino hospitality at its best was shown by the Cebuano hosts to their guests. Surely, for the majority of the delegates who came to Cebu for the first time, it was an experience and a privilege to see the cross of Magellan, walk Colon Avenue, pray at the shrine of Santo Niño, feel the Cebuano's devotion to their newly beatified Pedro Calungsod.

The Mission Congress celebration went very smoothly. After the opening day ceremonies highlighted by the Keynote Address of the Papal Legate and the other messages from other guests, the stress and strain caused by such an important event started to get colored with excitement and other expectations. The happy, festive atmosphere of the congress was contagious.

The Cebu Secretariat did an efficient and splendid work in running the whole affair, from Program Implementation, including the opening and closing ceremonies of the congress, the liturgy, the documentation, and exhibits—even extending to the physical and technical facilities, accommodation and transportation, and general logistics—and whatever other concerns fall under these categories.

The bishops set the tone for this mission congress: *awareness of our commitment to mission.* How ready are we as a local church to share the faith we have received? While the congress was supposed to be an expression of our faith as a local church and a renewal of our missionary commitment, perhaps what it primarily did was to give us the occasion as a people to look very honestly at our faith and faith convictions, to ask ourselves whether we feel the urgency for mission which comes only from a strong and living faith.

The participants of the First National Mission Congress, owning the Pastoral Letter on the Church's Mission in the Third Millennium issued by the CBCP last July 2000, affirmed the missionary nature of the Church, that every baptized person is missionary, that Jesus is our model missionary, and that we have to be missionaries both here at home and abroad.

The most moving and inspiring activity of the mission congress celebration was the "mission sending" ceremony. Fittingly, it capped a fruitful and happy celebration of our faith. Saint Francis of Assisi has said: "it is in giving that we receive." Let us share our faith so that it grows. Let us give and share what the Lord has given so we may get back more in return.

WORDS OF THANKS

As the overall coordinator of the National Mission Congress, I take this opportunity to express my sincere and lasting gratitude to those who helped make the National Mission Congress 2000 truly memorable and successful. While I am not able to name everyone in this acknowledgment, the Lord surely knows who they are.

I would like to thank most especially Father Catalino Arévalo, SJ, and Father James Kroeger, MM, for the support, sacrifice, and love-offering they willingly contributed to the Church for the success of the National Mission Congress. Father Arévalo's vast wealth of experience which he generously shares, his talent which he has given to the service of Church all his life and continues to share with others, but most of all for his availability to help and his humility, not only helped make the Congress truly successful; he inspired many of us without end. Father Kroeger, whose knowledge of missiology is rooted and enriched by his mission experience, contributed and continues to offer his expertise and service to the Church. The mission materials, *MARK* (prepared for the seminar-workshop of the bishops), and the ten modules for mission animation, *Tell the World...* are his work, for the service of the Philippine Church, for the mission.

To the members of the Episcopal Commission on Mission, Archbishop Gordoncillo and Bishops Camiña, Rillera, Galang, Amantillo who were always there to advise, support and encourage; to the other National Executive Committee members, Bishops Cabajog and John Du, Father Pete Mesiona, MSP, Monsignor P. Quitorio, Father Oscar Ante, OFM, and Mother Clarita Balleque, RVM, who were always ready and available to help; to the National Coordinating Secretariat, initially manned by Father Oliver Quilab, SVD (who had to report to his mission assignment in Germany), Sister Ma. Leonora A. Pataueg, MCJ and Sister Ma. Corazon O. Mercurio, FSP, who ably took over the Secretariat's work; and to the Cebu Coordinating Secretariat headed by Monsignor Esteban Binghay, Father Aquilino Tabamo, MSP, Father Terence Madden, Sister Cecilia Espenilla, OP, and Sister Ma. Felisa Declaro, RVM, who with their other staff did a tremendous job during the Congress proper, I am deeply grateful.

I express my gratitude to His Eminence Ricardo Cardinal Vidal, whose humble and affable ways inspired us all to make the event, that was the National Mission Congress, "Cebu 2000," truly memorable and successful.

I must thank His Excellency Archbishop Antonio Franco, for the concern, advice and help he offered in so many ways; he made my work and responsibility lighter.

My gratitude goes to my brother Bishops, for their trust and confidence in giving me the rare opportunity to serve the Church of the Philippines by organizing the First National Mission Congress. The support and encouragement you gave, I will always cherish. Heartfelt thanks goes to Archbishop Oscar Cruz, the President of the CBCP when the decision to hold the Mission Congress was made, and to Archbishop Orlando Quevedo, OMI, current President of the CBCP, for their support for the congress and their being a brother to me. What more could I ask for? Once again, sincere thanks!

CELEBRATING A
MISSION CONGRESS

Catalino G. Arévalo, SJ

T he Church exists to proclaim the Name of Jesus to the world. And thus, the ultimate purpose of Jubilee Year 2000 was to bring Jesus and his Gospel anew to a world that has either turned away from him, or—in Asia—has not really encountered him. Almost four billion Asians, as the Third Christian millennium opens, have not really met Christ in a significant way. It is the joyous task of Christians in Asia to proclaim the Name of Jesus to their fellow Asians, to make his Gospel known, by word, by witness and work, by worship.

Of the one hundred twenty-plus millions of Christians in Asia, nearly seventy millions are Filipinos. The third Christian millennium, which Pope John Paul II has perhaps prophetically named "the Asian millennium," thus challenges Filipino Christians as they have never been challenged before. The Holy Father has addressed these words to us: "I wish to tell you of my special desire· that the Filipinos will become the foremost missionaries of the Church in Asia."

In 1979 (2-7 December), Manila hosted the first International Congress on Mission held in Asia after the Second Vatican Council. This Congress, under the overall direction of then Auxiliary Bishop Gaudencio B. Rosales of Manila, brought together hundreds of delegates from all over Asia and all over the world to reflect on the task of Christian mission, specially in Asia, for the coming decades. In many ways it was an extraordinarily fruitful assembly, and by the grace of the Spirit, became a wellspring for mission-thinking, mission-renewal, mission-commitment, in the twenty years that were to follow.

When the Jubilee Year 2000 was being planned by the Catholic Bishops' Conference of the Philippines (CBCP), it was decided that one of the highpoints of the year's realization in our country was to be a National Mission Congress, to be organized by the Episcopal Commission on Missions of the CBCP under Bishop Vicente C. Manuel, SVD, chairman of the commission.

Choosing Cebu. For the site of the Congress, the CBCP chose the City of Cebu, a choice accepted with great generosity by His Eminence, Ricardo Cardinal Vidal, the cardinal-archbishop. Auxiliary Bishop Antonieto D. Cabajog would be the Cebu Officer-in-charge, greatly assisted by Bishop John F. Du and Monsignor Esteban S. Binghay. As it turned out, the choice of Cebu was not only right; it was inspired; it was providential. Cebu offered its resources—people-wise, treasure-wise, enthusiasm-wise, and with the Lord's abundant blessing, the week-long conference became a true festival of faith, became itself a missionary event. The Church of Cebu was challenged and taxed by all the demands of this project, and its leaders and its faithful rose superbly to the challenge.

Cebu is rightly called the cradle of the Christian faith in Asia. It was in Cebu that the faith was first planted in the Philippines; it was from Cebu that the Catholic faith began its speedy spread through the Philippines' many islands, many tribes, many communities. Some forty years after the first missionary labors began in Cebu, the Philippines had become "the beginnings of a Christian nation."

In the year 2000 also, Cebu was celebrating the beatification, on 5 March, of one of its sons, Pedro Calungsod. Calungsod belonged to the diocese of Cebu (we do not know where exactly he was born), and at the tender age of 13 or 14, accompanied the Jesuit Fathers who founded the first mission in the Marianas Islands in 1668. He left his homeland with perhaps 17 of his fellow-Filipinos to undertake mission work in the islands first named *Islas de los Ladrones* (Robbers' Islands). Calungsod did heroic labors there with the Spanish Jesuits. On 2 April 1672, side by side with Diego Luis de San Vitores, mission superior and saintly disciple of Christ, he was martyred at Tumhon beach, not far from today's Agaña in Guam.

It was only in the 1980s, centuries later, that Father San Vitores and Pedro

Calungsod were rescued from oblivion, and raised to the altars, Father San Vitores in 1985, Calungsod, in the first beatifications of the Jubilee Year 2000. The grace of Calungsod's beatification was very much part of the National Mission Congress in September 2000.

What happened in Cebu? The Cebu Congress was first of all a **celebration** of the Christian faith of the Filipino people. In some ways, so many participants testified, it was an "explosion" of the faith in their minds and hearts. One parish delegate from Manila said to one of the organizers, months later: "I had not expected to be so moved and my faith so greatly renewed. The Congress was a gift to me; it has already had a profound effect in my life as a Catholic."

What happened at Cebu? The Mission Congress intended to be itself "mission"—**catechesis** on the meaning of mission in the life of the Church and of all Christians. The conferences were thus geared to catechetical instruction and "conscientization" (awareness-raising) of the thousands of delegates and non-delegates who took part in the Congress proper.

Thus, the main assemblies and the workshops focused on the *theological bases and the concrete tasks of mission*, specially as developed in the papal texts, *Evangelii Nuntiandi* (Pope Paul VI), *Redemptoris Missio* (Pope John Paul II), and *Ecclesia in Asia* (also Pope John Paul II). *Ecclesia in Asia* was the Holy Father's own summing-up of the twenty-five years of common reflection of the Asian Bishops in the Federation of Asian Bishops' Conferences (FABC). Very much present in the reflection of organizers, speakers and participants was the CBCP's just-issued document on the Church in the Philippines and its mission vocation and task.

Even if the major themes on mission had been taken up in the 1979 International Mission Congress, it was thought that they should be taken up again, for the interval of twenty years had made them, if anything, more relevant, more urgent, and clearer, better understood—especially the great new area of mission reflection, *interreligious dialogue*.

Congress Content. Most of the general conferences were superbly given and really "communicated." Father Luis Antonio Tagle's "overall vision" of the meaning of proclaiming Jesus to Asia was profound and moving for so many. Fathers Bob McCahill and James Kroeger (both Maryknoll missioners) told mission-stories effectively and with much impact (their focus was interreligious dialogue). Father Daniel Patrick Huang, SJ ended the series of addresses with a superb presentation of the spirituality of mission.

Father Ruben Gomez, OMI very simply shared the story of Oblate mission in the Philippines, touching briefly but movingly on his OMI-brother, the lovable and saintly Bishop Benjamin de Jesus, who was slain in the pursuit of his missionary ministry. Father Pio Estepa, SVD spoke effectively on the process of inculturation with great clarity and pedagogical skill, and Father Luis Hechanova, CSsR addressed the concern for social transformation with his accustomed forcefulness. The *catechesis* was developed in the afternoon sessions given to audiences of delegates and Cebu-Catholics who were not able to attend the general sessions.

The liturgies were truly festive and impressive: the faithful filled them with their profound faith. In a way they would have wanted to participate more fully, joining in the songs and prayers especially, but it was difficult to find the right mix of what might be called "Roman-style solemnity" and the obvious longing of the people to take fuller and more joyous part in the ceremonies—all of them so moving and so beautifully done. [In the future perhaps more "popular" rites could be inserted into the program.]

The organizers also realized from the beginning that participation of women in the Congress needed "amplification." Plans to have Sister Nirmala, successor to Mother Teresa with the Missionaries of Charity, and another outstanding Asian woman missionary did not materialize. We were fortunate in having Mrs. Henrietta Tambunting de Villa, Philippine Ambassador to the Holy See and outstanding Catholic layperson give the "Preface" to the entire Congress. Mrs. Corazon Cojuangco Aquino, former President of the Philippines, and also an outstanding Catholic laywoman, spoke movingly on Christian witness as mission, as exemplified in the life, conversion, and death of her husband, Senator Benigno Aquino. Several workshops were directed by religious sisters and laywomen, all of them very rich in content and spirit.

The organizers had first intended to make the National Mission Congress a "Youth Mission Congress." This did not prove possible, mostly for financial reasons. Young people from our parishes could not afford the expenses of travel, board-and-lodging, and full participation in the five days of the conference. The young people of Cebu and elsewhere were part of every step of the Congress preparation and "happening," but a more active role would have been desirable. It is still our dream to have a "Youth Mission Congress" in the future, for—after all—who will be "sent," who will "go forth" from the Church in our country, but our young people, our wonderfully talented, creative, energetic, generous, loving young people? *Speriamo!*

The final event of the Mission Congress, the closing Mass presided over by His Eminence the Papal Legate, John Baptist Cardinal Wu, along with the mission-sending rites with the President of the CBCP, Archbishop Orlando Quevedo, "sending forth" the Philippine missioners present to their various missionary assignments, was—for all participants—the really high-point of the days of assembly, sharing and worship. All mission is **commitment and commission**, and this final dramatic "going forth" was "going forth" in deed and in truth, in obedience to the "great commission" of Jesus before his Ascension, his return to the Father.

What happened at Cebu? Did we realize what we wanted to bring about? As could be expected, we can say both *No* and *Yes.* There were many things we could have done and done better, but the whole country was already in the grip of a serious economic downturn, and this accounted for much of the "cutting down" that had to be done. The concerned bishops, priests and the faithful people—in Cebu, above all—did so much; they wanted to do even more, but their resources were not always equal to their generous hearts. [We cannot thank Bishop John F. Du and his associates sufficiently for all they gave for the success of the Congress!] But, the *Yes*-answer is to be given, loud and strong.

The Congress, with the abundant grace of the Lord, and surely by the intercession of Our Lady, Mother of Asian peoples and Queen of Missions, was a gift—truly a generous gift—to the Church in the Philippines, to the thousands of our faithful who helped, in a hundred ways, to "real-ize" the Congress, to prepare for it, to take care of the thousands of details that went into it, to bring it to gracious actualization—hour after hour, day after day.

Congress Commitments. We are sure that from the Cebu Congress, in ever-widening waves, the message of the Congress will reach every diocese and parish—and hopefully every Christian community in our land. We trust, with God's continuing help, that what the Congress wanted to proclaim, **will be proclaimed** in coming months and years throughout our country:

>>> The "hour of mission" is sounding, and sounding now, for the Church and faithful of the Philippines. A calling, that now comes to its fulfillment, has been there from the beginnings, but now—at the beginning of the third Chris-

tian millennium, "the Asian millennium"—it rings loud and clear and must be
heard by all.

>>> Every Catholic, every Christian is, by virtue of Baptism and Confirma-
tion, and by virtue of the Eucharist, truly a missionary, and must fulfill this Christian calling in every possible way open to him or her (not excluding children!):
by word, by worship, by witness, by work. No one may be excused from this
task, this mandate to mission.

>>> Mission begins where one is: at home, even within its walls (even
sick people have a missionary task cut out for them); in our neighborhood; in
all its circles of human contact and communication; in and through our parishes and Church communities; within every diocese.

>>> Mission is *at home*, for our modern and post-modern age is rapidly, all
too rapidly, secularizing and dechristianizing our Philippine culture and lifestyles,
especially in the milieu of our young people; the duty to proclaim Christ and
his Gospel in every possible way is an imperative (as never before!) in our own
land.

>>> Mission is *ad gentes*. Asia, the Asia of this new millennium, with its
four billion Asians, is at a moment of history where a new world is a-borning. It
will be born, it will emerge dramatically, with Jesus and his Gospel, or without
them: the *with* or *without* depends on us, under God. But in God's design, his
work of "bringing all things together" in Christ, this work God has made ours
also. And that work is *Mission in our time*, this time of crisis and challenge, this
millennium of Asia, where nearly four billion people, most of them, have not
heard the Good News of Jesus Christ!

Part Two

INTRODUCTIONS

CONGRESS MESSAGES

THE MESSAGE OF THE HOLY FATHER:

The Holy Father was pleased to be informed that the National Mission Congress will be held in Cebu from September 27 to October 1, 2000. On this occasion he sends warm greetings to all taking part and assures them of his prayers for the success of this event. Bearing witness to Christ is the supreme service which the Church can offer to the peoples of Asia.... His Holiness, therefore, encourages the Congress participants to develop initiatives, aimed at making the Person of Jesus Christ better known and loved by all Filipino Catholics in accordance with your theme: "Tell the World of His Love." Through prayers, catechesis, meditative reading of the Gospel and the Eucharistic adoration, it will be possible for many to rediscover the unsearchable riches of Christ who is the ultimate answer to the deepest yearning of the human heart.

Entrusting all present to the protection of Mary, Mother of the Redeemer, His Holiness cordially imparts his apostolic blessing....

CONGRESS MESSAGE TO THE HOLY FATHER:

The National Mission Congress of the Catholic Bishops' Conference of the Philippines, with His Eminence Cardinal John Baptist Wu, your holiness' legate to the Congress, and the entire Philippine Episcopal Conference, thank your holiness for the gracious message imparting your apostolic blessing on all of us gathered here in the City of Cebu.

Two thousand three hundred delegates—Bishops, priests and religious, and lay people—will study and reflect on our Lord's mandate on mission, His prayer for unity for all, in the light of your holiness' apostolic exhortation *Ecclesia in Asia* and your holiness' often repeated wish that Filipino Catholics be missionaries in Asia as the Third Christian Millennium opens... [and] as the entire Church in the Philippines re-dedicates herself to proclaiming Jesus and his Gospel and to "tell the world of His love."

MESSAGE FROM THE CONGREGATION FOR THE EVANGELIZATION OF PEOPLES (Josef Cardinal Tomko and Marcello Zago, OMI):

It gives me immense joy to send my prayerful wishes and warm greetings to all who are gathered in Cebu City to take part in the National Mission Congress.

When the entire Church celebrates the Great Jubilee of the Year 2000, all our attention is focused on the Person of Christ, the fullness of Divine Revelation. This definitive self-revelation of God in Christ is the fundamental reason why the Church is missionary by her nature. It is edifying to learn of this special effort taken by the local Church in the Philippines in organizing this Mission Congress....

While imploring God's choicest blessings on this eventful occasion, I am united with you in prayers for a special outpouring of the Holy Spirit for the successful outcome of this Mission Congress for the further growth of the Church in the Philippines and in Asia.

MESSAGE OF ORLANDO B. QUEVEDO, CBCP PRESIDENT:

"Tell the world of His love!" These words from the official song of the 1995 World Youth Day in Manila summarize the mission of the Church. The words speak of proclaiming Jesus Christ to the world. They urge us to tell the world of the extraordinary love that impelled Jesus to suffer and to offer his life on the Cross for the salvation of the world. There "is no greater love than this." By such love Jesus became the Savior of the world.

The National Mission Congress in Cebu City on September 27 to October 1, 2000 will reflect on and discuss the many aspects of mission in our world, especially in the Philippines and in Asia. Proclamation, human promotion, inculturation, interreligious dialogue, ecumenism, and spirituality—these are the major dimensions of mission that the Congress will treat.

We all wish to know what Jesus meant when he said, "As the Father has sent me, so I am sending you" (John 20:21) and when he said, "Be witnesses to what you have seen and heard" (Luke 24:46-48). The National Mission Congress will catechize us, educate us, form us, and encourage us to develop a vibrant missionary spirit....

We pray that at the beginning of the Third Millennium, in this Year of the Great Jubilee, the Congress would usher in a new missionary era in the Philippines for our own land and for Asia. We pray, "Here we are, Father, send us in your Name."

MESSAGE OF RICARDO J. CARDINAL VIDAL:

With sentiments of great joy, I welcome all the delegates and participants to the first-ever National Mission Congress. Indeed, the Archdiocese of Cebu takes pride of the privilege given to us of hosting this historic event of the Church in the Philippines on the occasion of the Great Jubilee Year.

...It was here in Cebu that the seed of Christianity in the Philippines was first sown more than four hundred years ago. Since then, our Catholic faith has become intricately woven into our history as a nation until now. ...we come back to Cebu on this occasion of the National Mission Congress for us to sow seeds once more—so that we may be able to continue to proclaim, promote, and live meaningfully our Christian faith vis-à-vis the contemporary world....

It is not mere coincidence that in this Year of the Great Jubilee, the Holy Father raised into the dignity of the altars Blessed Pedro Calungsod, a young missionary and catechist who was martyred for his Christian faith in Guam in 1672.

Blessed Pedro Calungsod was a "noble son" of the Church of Cebu. In this National Mission Congress, he becomes our model and example of a true missionary to all the delegates and participants of the Congress....

WELCOME REMARKS

BISHOP VICENTE C. MANUEL, SVD:

...Today, we are gathered to celebrate the first ever National Mission Congress, as a fitting culminating activity to end the three years of intense preparation for the Great Jubilee of the year 2000. This signal event is our first step as a Local Church into the Third Millennium, "to undertake a life-task for this *kairos*, this hour of grace given us as the People of God journeying with our Asian brothers and sisters toward his Kingdom" (*Pastoral Letter on Mission*, 5 July 2000).

"Rejoice in the Lord, I say it again, rejoice," St. Paul exhorted the Philippians. Let joy and rejoicing in the Lord be the pervading atmosphere and integrating mood of this congress....

Two important mission-related events preceded this congress; the first was the journey throughout the country of the relic of Saint Therese of the Child Jesus, the universal patroness of mission. Last March, Pedro Calungsod was beatified. Are these not reasons for rejoicing? Our rejoicing is our way of thanking the Lord.

During this congress we will focus on the Church and the task of evangelization, the main mission and vocation proper to the Church. Through concrete experiences, the Jesus-story will be retold to us by missionaries from at home and abroad. They will narrate to us how they proclaimed Jesus in different life situations, among peoples of different faiths and cultures, among the destitute and marginalized. They will share how they proclaimed Jesus by their witness of life, by their presence, by listening—through dialogue....

After everything shall have been said and done, we can only say, "we are unworthy servants, we did only what we were supposed to do." After all, it is the work of the Holy Spirit, the principal agent of mission. Thank you.

BISHOP ANTONIETO D. CABAJOG:

Malipayong pag-abut! Today we gather as a "community of disciples," sharers in the mission of Christ. We come together by the Spirit to, first and foremost, retell the story of Jesus Christ, with a yearning and desire so ardent and deep that, through this act of retelling, our hearts will be "on fire with the love of Christ and burning with zeal to make him known more widely, loved more deeply, and followed more closely" (EA 23).

As bearers of Christ's joy, we are invited to recount our own experiences of missionary work, our sharing in the joy and hope, the grief and anguish of the men and women of today, for us to be brought to a profound realization that our stories as pilgrims have undoubtedly bonded and bound us as God's people striving to respond to the palpable movements of Christ in our history. And though we may have varied and, even sometimes conflicting, experiences in our pilgrimage, our belief is that God has already begun His work of synthesizing our accounts into one beautiful story—God's love story with his creatures.

Our gathering is, moreover, a gathering to discern how we can more effectively retell the story of Jesus in this generation that "puts more trust in witnesses than in teachers, in experience than in teaching, in life and action than in theories," in a context "where people are more persuaded by holiness of life than by intellectual argument" (EA 42).

May this National Mission Congress, the first ever in this Christian country, renew our commitment to retell the story of Jesus....

INTRODUCTIONS TO THE CONGRESS

AMBASSADOR HENRIETTA T. DE VILLA:

Maayong hapon. God is kind. God is truly kind. I thought I'd never make it to Cebu.... That I am here, that you—each and every one of you—are here for this First National Mission Congress is proof of God's loving concern....

Over a year ago, Bishop Manuel was in Rome and he gave me a letter inviting me to this First National Mission Congress as one of its five presidents. Oh, I was so thrilled and excited—and not really because of the "president" portion of the invitation. I was so excited because any event of the Church I love, any happening, whether in joy or anguish, of the people of God of our country evokes such a stirring in my heart that has not diminished in spite of the distance and the years....

The process for the Cause of Pedro Calungsod as a servant of God worthy to be raised to the honor of the altar formally began only in 1994. Up until early 1999, his Cause did not seem to stand a chance for early approval in the Vatican.... Pedro Calungsod, a virtual unknown, an obscure Cebuano who was merely a boy, what chance did he have to be declared a martyr on the great Jubilee 2000?

But we believed. Oh, how we believed that it could happen because nothing is impossible with God. And we prayed, believing that prayer is the weakness of God. And we worked, hoping for a manifestation that God always pitches his tent with the obscure and marginalized. There was Cardinal Vidal, the gentle shepherd with the eagle's foresight, dreaming, planning, charting the path to Pedro Calungsod's beatification. There was Father Ildebrando Leyson, who can now be called Father "Ildepedro" Leyson, patiently and tenaciously outlining the path of his martyrdom. And there were people in the Vatican, starting with our cherished Holy Father Pope John Paul II, who saw the significance in raising Pedro Calungsod as a model of holiness and an exemplar of mission for the young and old, for the women and men of this millennium....

And so, behold Beato Pedro Calungsod, Bisaya from Cebu, the virtual unknown, dashing from behind and making it to the frontline of beatifications and canonizations for the Jubilee year. How obvious the Lord's preferential love for the poor—in their weakness, his strength shines forth....

It was not by chance that the beatification of blessed Pedro Calungsod, a young catechist, missionary and martyr, happened in this Jubilee year. As it is not by chance that the First National Mission Congress happens here in Cebu where the seed of faith was first planted in our land. It is all about mission. It is all about God calling us more emphatically in this Jubilee Year....

No one is exempt from missionary work. Pope John Paul II, the Holy Father we love, whose back is now bent by the years of labor, but whose energy is ever young, ever new, calls and calls and still calls to the Church and to the world, "Open the doors to Christ." And, our Second Plenary Council in 1991 has put the Philippine Church in a state of mission and outlined the wider coverage this mission now entails. And, by the Philippine Church, we mean all the people of God of our country....

Only when Christ has touched our faith and touched our heart can we touch the faith and the heart of others. "In the end, everything begins up there and ends down here with love." Like Pedro Calungsod, we can and will make disciples of all nations when we love and love and love some more....

ARCHBISHOP CHARLES A. SCHLECK, CSC:

I wish to begin by expressing my deep thanks to Archbishop Quevedo, the President of the Philippine Bishops' (Episcopal) Conference and to the other organizers of this Mission Congress, for extending to me an invitation to participate in the proceedings of this extremely significant event as the representative of the Cardinal Prefect of the Congregation for the Evangelization of Peoples.... My reason for being with you here these days is to express the profound gratitude of the Congregation for the Evangelization of Peoples to the Church in the Philippines for the missionary service which you have provided for the world. The Catholic Church in your country represents some 85% or more of its entire population, thus one would expect to receive from this large number of persons, perhaps the greatest possible force for assisting the Church in Asia in fulfilling its missionary responsibility *ad gentes*: that is to bring Christ to Asia and Asia to Christ....

This requires many apostles who are willing to spend themselves in the service of the Lord, even should this require the sacrifice of their lives as was true of so many Asian martyrs, like Saint Lorenzo Ruiz and his companions whose feast we celebrate tomorrow and the recently beatified Pedro Calungsod. It is no secret that the presence of thousands of Filipinos and Filipinas throughout the world has been at the same time, an extremely important contribution to the missionary efforts of the Church, and above all to the Church's being more capable of responding to the Lord's mandate given to the entire Church: "Go and make disciples of all nations, baptizing them in the name of the Father and of the Son and of the Holy Spirit" (Matthew 28:19-20).

The present Assembly or Congress, is another testimony of the desire on the part of the Philippine Church to deepen, to renew and to further its *missionary* commitment to the life of the Church, not only in regard to your own country, which continues to have missionary dioceses *ad gentes*, but also in regard to the Church in Asia and elsewhere throughout the world. The Holy Father indicated in the Encyclical *Redemptoris Missio*, that the Church all over the world in the Third Millennium must turn its attention to this Continent, where the Son of God was born in our human flesh and chose to initiate the work of salvation which the Father had sent him to undertake in the fullness of time.

As the Holy Father mentioned in the Apostolic Exhortation, *Ecclesia in Asia*, it remains a mystery why the Savior of the world, born in this Continent, has until now remained largely unknown to its people. And yet, given the command which the Son of God received from the Father in his mandate to become one of us, "if the Church in Asia is to fulfill its providential destiny, Evangelization as the joyful, patient and progressive preaching of the saving Death and Resurrection of Jesus Christ *must be your absolute priority*" (Address of John Paul II, FABC VI)....

The reasons for this urgency and priority in regard to the proclamation of Jesus as the one and only Savior of the world sent by the Father are many. Despite the fact that this Continent is home to over 60% of the world's population, in your Bishops' Pastoral Letter *Missions and the Church in the Philippines* of July 5, 2000, they stated that the total number of those who profess the Catholic faith in Asia comes to about 125 million Catholics, of whom some 70 million live in the Philippines.... In this same Continent are to be found about 85% of the non-Christians of the world. Whence it is no wonder that the Holy Father, just ten years ago in the Encyclical *Redemptoris Missio*, on six occasions insisted that the mission *ad gentes* would have to address itself *especially* to Asia, to the Continent where you yourselves are living, in the Third Millennium....

PAPAL LEGATE JOHN BAPTIST CARDINAL WU:

The Second Vatican Council urged us all, in different ways, to return to our origins in order to understand who we are and where we are going. A Congress devoted to the theme of Mission must, then, return to the *source* of *all* mission in the Church: "as the Father has sent me, so I send you" (John 20:21). Sent by the Father, Jesus is the source of our mission. We return, then, to Jesus, for our inspiration and model, for the theological source of all our reflection. We return to Jesus to renew our vision of what mission is and what it may become in the years ahead.

In the last twenty years or so, theologians have recovered, perhaps rediscovered, the ways in which story-telling is a very powerful Biblical instrument for conveying divine truth. Narrative theology has been established as a fruitful exegetical and hermeneutic instrument. Through the stories of both the Old and New Testaments, we learn to share more fully in God's vision for the world.

It is a felicitous thought, then, that for this Mission Congress the organizers have chosen the topic of storytelling, a topic to be explored in talks and specialized workshops, accompanied by sessions in which the aim will be a theological deepening of the theme of *mission*.

The topic is timely, for, if we return to Jesus as the source of mission, narrative theology calls to our attention the fact that Jesus was a story-teller. Asked the somewhat theoretical question, "Who is my neighbor?" Jesus replied with the story of *The Good Samaritan* (Luke 10:30-37). In seeking to get the Pharisees to change their minds and accept a different way of looking at God, a new vision for the work of the Messiah, Jesus told the story of *The Return of the Prodigal Son* (Luke 15:11-32).

The topic of story-telling also provides this Mission Congress with an important methodology for reflection, for missionaries have always told the story of their experience in preaching the Gospel. At the Council of Jerusalem, Peter told the story of his encounter with Cornelius. On his visits to Jerusalem, Paul recounted the story of the way in which the Gentiles received the faith. Francis Xavier wanted to run through the Universities of Europe, telling the story of his encounter with Asia and its millions of people waiting to receive the liberating truth of Christ.... Missionaries returned to their homelands, bringing with them vivid and inspiring stories, which could light the flame of evangelizing in young hearts.

Narrative theology has taught us to look at the whole art of story-telling in the Bible. As an important by-product of this enterprise, we are encouraged to look more deeply into all the other stories which are part of our lives—the story of our own personal faith journey—the stories embedded in our own cultures. Exploring these stories, we are led to a new and inspiring encounter with truth. We have discovered that the greatest stories are journey stories, and that the most significant journey stories are stories of homecoming. We think of the story of Exodus; we think of *The Return of the Prodigal Son....* All this is so true that someone has very perceptively said: "You cannot tell people what to do; you can only tell them parables."

...as the Papal Legate to this National Mission Congress, I wish you no less than this desire of the Holy Father. May the story of your faith, hope and love in Christ be an authentic and fruitful *new* recital of the *logos* of the Cross (I Corinthians 1:18), of the story of Jesus crucified and risen (Colossians 1:24). May the *story* of your Congress tell the *dream* of this new civilization of love. God bless you all.

Part Three

CONGRESS

PICTORIAL

MISSION CONGRESS MEMORIES

Opening ceremonies participants: O. Quevedo, C. Schleck, J.B. Wu, R. Vidal, H. de Villa.

National Executive Committee members: A. Cabajog, J. Kroeger, V. Manuel.

Opening Eucharist: F. Kriekenbeek, A. Franco, E. Khong Kin Cheun, C.G. Arévalo, J.B. Wu.

Registration
at the Congress.

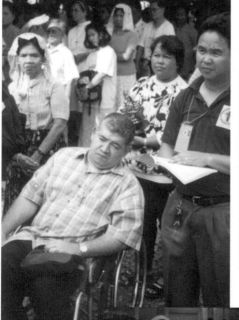

Welcome to Cebu, home of
Señor Santo Niño.

Participants at
Eucharistic
celebration.

Youth
participants
at the
Congress.

Bob McCahill
listens to a friend.

Words of congratulation: A. Franco and L. Tagle.

Two speakers: D. Huang
and O. Quevedo.

Introducing a speaker:
P. Mesiona.

Some delegates from Manila:
E. Eusebio, C. Durano,
A. Dy, J. Kroeger.

Prayer and
song leaders.

Bishop participants:
P. Alo, M. Sobreviñas,
J. Salazar, A. Ledesma.

Charismatic prayer
at the Congress.

One of
twenty
specialized
workshops.

Bishops chat while
preparing for Eucharist:
I. Amantillo, A. Bastes,
G. Camiña, C. Cenzon.

Cardinal Jaime L. Sin
preaches at Eucharist.

Friends meeting in Cebu:
Sr. M. Balleque and C.G. Arévalo.

Corazon C. Aquino
addresses the assembly.

Doctoral awardees:
E. Malone, C. Schleck.

Bishops enjoy
the barrio fiesta:
J. Du, J. Baylon,
S. Balce.

Evening entertainment: Bishops
S. Utleg, L. Medroso, A. Rañola.

Seminarians enjoy
the lechon.

Congress
staff members
in offertory
procession.

Concelebrants
after closing
Eucharist.

Reliquary
of Mission
Saints:
L. Ruiz,
Thérèse,
P. Calungsod,
F. Xavier.

The ever-affable Cardinal Vidal.

**Friends gather with
Msgr. E. Binghay.**

**C. Schleck
with
B. Bernardo
of media team.**

**Scene from drama
on Calungsod's life.**

**Returning statue
after congress
concludes.**

Part Four

ADDRESSES

AND

PRESENTATIONS

MISSION: A THEOLOGICAL OVERVIEW

Luis Antonio G. Tagle

There are many ways of viewing and explaining mission. The history of the Church attests to shifts in its understanding and practice [1]. It is therefore quite legitimate for us to explore the meaning of mission from the perspective provided by our immediate context which is that of the Jubilee of the Year 2000, its grace and demands. Since the Great Jubilee celebrates the Incarnation of the Word of God, it is interesting to see how a theological view of mission will emerge when this mystery of the Christian faith is chosen as its main interpretative key.

I. The Mystery of the Incarnation and Mission. To begin with, let us consider a few scriptural texts that deal with the Incarnation [2].

Galatians 4:4-5: "When the fullness of time had come, God sent forth the Son, born of woman, born under the law to redeem those who were under the law, so that we might receive adoption as children." We have here a qualitative view of time that allows us to see it as possessing fullness, and presumably emptiness. Time is what subjects endowed with freedom do with it. In this case, time happens in the dialogical interaction between God and humankind. The fullness of time, which comes with the sending of the Son born of woman, coincides with the fullness of God's loving self-communication. This in turn makes of men and women children of God who is revealed as *Abba*. The incarnation fulfills time through God's self-revelation in love and the unfolding of the filial identity of men and women.

Colossians 1:15, 19-20: "He is the image of the invisible God, the first-born of all creation. For in him all the fullness of God was pleased to dwell and through him to reconcile to himself all things, whether on earth or in heaven." One of the deepest desires of the human heart is to see God. In our time marked by so much suffering, people often ask where they could find God. The Christian faith declares that Jesus, as the incarnation of the Word of God, is the visible image of the unseen God. But, the God revealed in Jesus does not always match our conventional notions of God. Thus, the incarnation provides us with a revelation of God that surprises, shocks and disturbs.

John 3:16-17: "For God so loved the world that He gave His only Son, that whoever believes in him should not perish but have eternal life. For God sent the Son into the world, not to condemn the world but that the world might be saved through him." On the one hand, the sending of the Son reveals God as a loving Father, whose desire is to save and not to condemn. On the other hand, the mission of the Son also reveals humanity as his own home (John 1:11), as children loved by the Father in the Son.

The three texts we have chosen depict the incarnation as a two-fold revelation. God and "God's world" are disclosed to us in a new way. Humanity and our world are at the same time revealed to us in a new light. Both movements happen in the person of the Incarnate Word, Jesus. Through Jesus, God is known in humanity and humanity is known in God. This double and concomitant revelation is made possible and even inevitable by the fact that Jesus is truly God and truly human. The Scriptural faith in the incarnation, affirmed by the Councils of Nicaea (325) and Chalcedon (451), is not only about the person of Jesus but also about the revelation of God that comes hand in hand with the revelation of what humanity is in God. As a framework for understanding mission, the mystery of the incarnation directs Christian mission towards disclosing the face of God and that of humanity as known in Jesus.

II. The Incarnation: Mission of Solidarity. It is not adequate to view the incarnation simply as the assumption of the eternal Word of a human body and form. God did not merely become human. The incarnation "shows the depth of God's involvement" [3], of God's total engagement in the lives and histories of human beings. The incarnation reveals a God who is not distant from humanity but one who is near and in solidarity with humanity, especially the poor and little ones. This is easily verified in how Jesus worked out his mission in identification with men and women in their specific life conditions, their longings, sufferings, failures and hopes.

John Paul II stated in *Ecclesia in Asia*: "He was close to the poor, the forgotten and the lowly, declaring that they were truly blessed, for God was with them. He ate with sinners, assuring them that at the Father's table there was a place for them when they turned from their sinful ways and came back to him. Touching the unclean and allowing them to touch him, he let them know the nearness of God. He wept for a dead friend, he restored a dead son to his widowed mother, he welcomed children, and he washed the feet of his disciples. Divine compassion has never been so immediately accessible" (11).

On account of the total involvement of God in humanity through the incarnation, the Reign of God, the central message of Jesus' mission, took different forms, depending on the varying situations of peoples [4]. In his encounter with those possessed by demonic powers, the Reign of God meant liberation. For the rich man searching for perfection, it meant dispossession of riches for the sake of the poor. For tax collectors, it meant restitution. For a widow in grief, it meant the gift of a son brought back to life. For a crucified criminal cognizant of his sins, it meant the promise of paradise. In other words, Jesus allows God to be known and heard within the experiences of people in a way that is uniquely personal to them. In whatever situation they may find themselves, God gets involved with them and utters a saving word to them. Using a variety of methods and expressions, Jesus, the Incarnate Word reveals God as *Abba*, the faithful Father of love and compassion.

As Jesus makes God known as *Abba*, he also makes known in surprising ways that human beings are truly children of God and in God, brothers and sisters, to one another. The nearness of God as the Father is accompanied by our nearness to one another in universal brotherhood and sisterhood. Jesus breaks down walls separating people from one another in the very same act that he reveals the identity of God as Father. Thus, knowing God as Father reverses the dehumanizing trends that have made human beings blind to the dignity of their brothers and sisters. Seeing God as close to humans enables humans to be close to one another. God's solidarity with us and solidarity among humans meet in the Word of God made human.

This aspect of the mystery of the incarnation spells out some directions for the understanding and exercise of the Church's mission. We indicate a few:

A. The mission of the Church rests on proclaiming by witness of life, word, relationships and structures, God and God's reign. It is important however, to ask what type of God is being proclaimed. The Incarnate Word proclaims a God of solidarity. But proclamation does not solely focus on God. Proclamation includes as an indispensable component the message about what humanity is all about. No true proclamation about God occurs without a corresponding proclamation about the truth of humanity in God.

B. Mission work is not only to be tied with a geographic space but with human space [5]. The "human landscape" is the true locale of mission. If we take Asia as an example, mission invites the Church not to enter "territories" but to enter human lives. Mission is "a walking into a people" that is so often described in *Ecclesia in Asia* as a people with a deep thirst, hunger and longing for life in order to make that thirst, hunger and longing our own.

C. Just as the Incarnate Word of God brought the Reign of God into various situations of peoples in a variety of expressions and methods, the Church needs to be untiring in its search for new expressions and new methods, as insisted upon by John Paul II. As humanity changes, new ways of unfolding the Reign of God are called forth. But these are discovered not through merely strategic planning but through journeying and solidarity with changing humanity.

D. Inculturation receives new impetus in this incarnational framework. The basic insight of Paul VI in *Evangelii Nuntiandi* rings more true. The mission of evangelization aims to bring the good news of salvation to all strata of human existence, ranging from human consciences to societal structures. This penetration of the saving message can happen only if the Church follows the incarnate Word that brought the Reign of God to all strata of human existence.

E. The promotion of human dignity, the recognition of universal brotherhood, peace-making and forging of dialogue become an imperative also. When the Church takes seriously its mission of proclaiming salvation as becoming children of an *Abba* who is in communion with us, then salvation includes people treating each other as brothers and sisters. From this perspective, Geneviève Comeau states that mission is "*filialiser le monde*," making the world a place for brothers and sisters [6]. Gustavo Gutierrez calls it a permanent exigency on the part of the Church to make universal communion happen [7].

As can be seen quite clearly, the implications we have indicated correspond to the triple direction of mission identified by the Special Assembly of the Synod of Bishops for Asia and the post-synodal apostolic exhortation *Ecclesia in Asia*, namely proclamation, communion and dialogue, and service of human promotion.

III. The Incarnation: Mission in Self-Emptying. The Incarnation of the Word happened in insignificance and hiddenness. This *kenosis* or self-emptying of the Word who did not deem equality with God something to be grasped at (Philippians 2:6-11) is proposed as a model for all followers of Jesus. This is the mind that we must take on, a "kenotic mind," one that embraces the lowly state and poverty of being human. It is in that lowly human form that the powerful God is known.

The *kenosis* that marks the very mystery of the Incarnation is verified in the different aspects of the life and mission of Jesus. The anonymity of the life in Nazareth, the non-messianic style of his public ministry and his death by condemnation are the significant manifestations in life of the "principle" of self-emptying of the Incarnation [8]. Jesus reveals the all-powerful God as one who refuses to employ divine power and glory. Christian Duquoc therefore describes the self-emptying of the Son as "revealing the divine in the form of its contrary" [9]. This inversion of God's image through *kenosis* frustrated people's expectations of easy social and political miracles coming from the hands of Jesus.

The *kenosis* of the Son in the incarnation is part of the "pedagogy" of the Trinitarian God as revealed in history. The incarnation of the Son is a moment in the *kenosis* of the Trinity. The Trinity is a self-effacing God, a God who gives all without any thought for getting any honor in return. God is a God who lets others be and respects their freedom even when used against the divine will. God does not conquer evil and hostility by a display of divine grandeur and power but by patient faithful mercy and love. Most especially in Jesus, God who is King is Father and Servant. In the Incarnate Son, God exercises divine power through solidarity with the suffering and the victims of society. "For because he himself has suffered and been tempted, he is able to help those who are tempted" (Hebrews 2:18).

The kenotic character of the incarnation does not only reveal who God is. It also exposes the falsehood, the uselessness and illusions of worldly ambitions.

It clearly manifests that unbridled human drives for success, power, popularity and achievement, extolled as marks of human fulfillment, often enslave us and make us enslave others. The kenotic incarnation of the Son makes us see that being human means stripping ourselves of all pretensions of grandeur. Being human is achieved in self-giving that does not count the cost, in letting others live, in conquering evil by good. A kenotic God is seen in kenotic humans. In *kenosis*, we see the true face of God and the true face of humanity.

Some implications of this aspect of the incarnation for mission need to be indicated now:

A.   For the Church everywhere, but most especially in Asia where most people live in poverty and oppression, mission is best served when it has emptied itself. David Bosch said, "As I see it, the hardest lesson the Church-in-mission will have to learn in the coming years is how to become again what it originally was, and always supposed to be: the Church without privileges, the Church of the catacombs, rather than of the halls of fame and power and wealth" [10].

B.   Mission is servanthood. Christians are called to be symbols of the self-effacing God they believe in and of the true spirit of humanity that Jesus reveals. Mission cannot stand on self-preservation for it is only in losing one's life that one finds it. Can the Church risk losing much of itself?

C.   The *kenosis* of the Son includes solidarity with victims, a solidarity that made him the saving High Priest. The mission of the Church is also promoted when the Church identifies itself with the victims of society and history. Felix Wilfred tells us that the poor are the best teachers of hope. "Like the lotus flower blossoming from out of the muddy bottom, the blooming of hope for the new century comes from the poor and their agenda" [11]. He claims that the future of humanity comes from the agenda of those in the periphery or margins rather than from the ambitions of those in the center. Can the Church empty itself to be with those in the periphery in its missionary enterprise?

D.   The *kenosis* of the Incarnate Son is mysteriously presented in his silence at his trial and death. It is not the silence of a helpless victim but that of someone living in dark faith. The Church's mission needs this silent contemplative stance. It cannot pretend to know all things, to have answers to all queries and to be in command over mystery. Mission is also served when the Church surrenders to mystery in naked silence.

E. Mission also must unveil to humanity its dehumanizing illusions. But the Church must be purged of its own illusions of power and wealth. Sean Kelly proposes an *"illusionectomy"* for the Church in every age [12]. If it wants to be truly missionary in the kenotic spirit of the Incarnate Word, then it must undergo also the painful process of purifying itself of its illusion. If the Church is to have any ambition, the only one justified "is to continue Jesus' mission of service and love, so that all [Asians] 'may have life and have it abundantly' (John 10:10)" [13].

IV. The Genesis of Christian Mission and the Figure of the Missioner. We close our reflection by asking how the mission of the Church was born. If there is one text from the New Testament that can paint a simple but vivid picture, it is the first letter of John 1:1-4 [14]. In this text, the apostle or proclaimer of Jesus as the Christ is one who has seen, touched, heard the Word of life who has been incarnated. The apostle desires to share this experience with a brother so that communion between them may be fostered. This human communion, according to the text, is actually communion with the Father and His Son, the Incarnate One.

When taken as a description of the beginning of the mission of the early Church, we can say that mission originated from a living and powerful experience of Jesus. The vocation of an apostle or one who is sent begins with an experience of Jesus. But what does an experience consist in? To experience Jesus is to touch the God that he reveals and the new humanity that he manifests. The original followers of Jesus saw, touched and heard in the very person of Jesus both God and humanity revealed in a new light. This experience is so powerful that it transformed timid, selfish and sinful men and women into great missioners and even martyrs for mission.

Who then is the missioner? The missioner is one who has experienced mission incarnated in the person of Jesus. The missioner is one who allows one's life, identity and work to be reshaped by that experience of God and of humanity in the Incarnate Word. Just as Jesus, the Missioner par excellence, brings together in his person the reality of God and of humanity that he reveals, so every missioner carries within his or her person the experience of God and of humanity in Jesus Christ. Like Jesus, the great lover of *Abba* and of God's children, missioners are given new fervor by falling in love with *Abba* and by believing in the promise of a new humanity. But like Jesus, true missioners must incarnate in the God and humanity they proclaim.

The Church has seen a host of valiant men and women who have served the cause of mission precisely by living according to the principle of the Incarnation of the Word. Our own Church in the Philippines can boast of San Lorenzo Ruiz and Blessed Pedro Calungsod. We have many Christians in Asia that quietly but persistently pursue mission because by not doing so, they would betray the God they have come to love and many brothers and sisters for whom they would gladly offer their lives. We have Fathers Jessie Palileo and Rhoel Gallardo, former students of mine, who by dying brought love of God and of neighbor in an unbreakable bond. And who would not be moved by the testimony of the Jesuit scholastic, Ritchie Fernando, who prayed to the God he loves that he might be found worthy to die for the poor he has come to love?

The Jubilee Year of the Incarnation teaches us that mission has a face and a name. Mission is Jesus, the Incarnate One. Mission is Jesus, the revealer of God and of the depths of humanity. Jesus is mission! May I become mission! May the Church truly be mission! In us, may God be known! In us, may a new humanity dawn!

---

[1] A good description of these shifts is given in Severino Dianich, *Chiesa in missione. Per una ecclesiologia dinamica*. Milano: Edizioni Paoline, 1985: 17-29.

[2] In the contemporary context of theology in Asia, the Incarnation has been the focus of creative and courageous reinterpretations. The best example is the work of Michael Amaladoss, S.J. See his "The Mystery of Christ and Other Religions:An Indian Perspective," *Vidyajyoti* 63 (1999): 327-338 and "Jésus Christ, the seul Sauveur, et la mission," *Spiritus* 61 (2000): 148-157.

[3] Sean P. Kelly, C.S.Sp., "Jesus' Approach to Mission," *African Ecclesial Review* 41 (1999): 66.

[4] *Ibid.*, 69.

[5] Gustavo Gutierrez said, "On a dit que cette mission avait été pensée uniquement en lien avec les espaces géographiques sans tenir compte des espaces humains." See "Mission et signes des temps," *Spiritus* 41 (2000): 184.

[6] Geneviève Comeau, "Le salut en Christ dans un contexte de pluralité religieuse," *Spiritus* 41 (2000): 146-147.

[7] Gutierrez, "Mission et signes des temps," 184.

[8] Christian Duquoc, "Discrétion du Dieu trinitaire et mission chrétienne," *Lumière et vie* 44: (2000): 80.

[9] "Kénotique, révéler le divin sous son contraire," *Ibid.*, p. 83.

[10] Quoted in Kelly, "Jesus' Approach to Mission," 71.

[11] Felix Wilfred, "The Agenda of the Victims.The Poor Explore the Hopes for a New Century" *Jeevadhara* 30 (2000): 7.

[12] Kelly, "Jesus' Approach to Mission," 70.

[13] *Ecclesia in Asia* 50.

[14] The theologian who uses this text creatively to explain the genesis of Christian mission is Severino Dianich. See his *Chiesa estroversa. Una ricerca sulla svolta dell'ecclesiologia contemporanea*. Milano: Edizioni Paoline, 1987.

Proclaiming Jesus Christ
The One Redeemer
Of The World

Ruben M. Gomez, OMI

My brothers and sisters, today I would like to tell you some stories about how the Oblates of Mary Immaculate have tried with the help of God's Spirit to *proclaim Jesus Christ the One Mediator and Sole Redeemer of Humankind* to people—Christians, Muslims, *Lumad*, and others—in Cotabato, Sulu, and Tawi-Tawi.

Beginnings. The late Bishop Gerard Mongeau, OMI, first bishop and then first archbishop of Cotabato, was superior of the Oblate scholasticate in Texas in 1939. His Provincial called him one day. "Father Mongeau, the General wants you to lead the first batch of Oblates to start a mission in the Philippines." Father Mongeau was surprised but deeply delighted by this opportunity for foreign mission. "Do you accept?" the Provincial asked. With his usual enthusiasm Father Mongeau answered, "Well, yes, of course, Father!" "Excellent," the Provincial was satisfied to end the conversation. But as an afterthought he asked Mongeau, "By the way, Father, do you have any questions for now?" After a few seconds Father Mongeau said, "By the way, Father, where is the Philippines?" That typical Mongeau enthusiasm and boldness were the guiding energy of the Oblate Missionary work in the next 50 years.

Of the seven Oblates who first arrived in Manila in 1939, Father Mongeau went to Cotabato and three went to Jolo. They were taking over from the Jesuits who had been in Jolo since 1748 and in Cotabato since 1862. And so you see, everything should be fine and under control! Other Oblates came from the States in 1940.

However, at this time, encouraged by the government's "Land for the Landless Program," about 600 to 800 settlers from Luzon and the Visayas were emigrating every month to the "Land of Promise." So, the Oblates arrived in midst of about 100,000 Catholics in the entire province of Cotabato. These were spread all over the land area of today's four big provinces—Maguindanao, Sultan Kudarat, North Cotabato and South Cotabato. They were four Oblates to take care of these areas. However, if any of these first companions felt that they could not do it (i.e. to minister to so many in so vast a territory), they decided not to tell Father Mongeau anymore. His standard answer to complaining Oblates was: "If you think you cannot do it then step aside and give way to somebody who is already doing it."

Being with the People—Journeying with Them. Although this situation happened almost by accident, being very close to the poor and to journeying people everywhere in Cotabato, Sulu, and Tawi-Tawi became a trademark of the Oblates. Right from the beginning, they proclaimed the faith to people whose life they shared and fairly understood. Let me tell you a story.

Sometime in 1942, Japanese soldiers arrested two Americans in Jolo, Fathers Emile Bolduc and Bernard Clancy. They were brought to the town plaza to be hanged or shot—whichever was "better." Father Bolduc wrote in his diary, "There was a Japanese soldier who had his gun ready to shoot us anytime. I thought to myself, *'Tapos na'!'* " But suddenly a Japanese—and old-timer in Jolo—came through the crowd and pleaded with the officers: "No! No!" And pointing to Father Bolduc, he assured the Japanese: "Good man! Good man!" Father Bolduc recognized him instantly. Although not a Catholic, that man was one among many who were deeply consoled by Father Bolduc's joyful, unassuming visits with people, especially the sick and the lonely—just because they were people, beloved brothers and sisters.

This closeness to the people has another version. From the time Father Primo Hagad was ordained an Oblate priest in 1957, it was clear that his mind and heart were filled with people's struggle for freedom, well-being, and survival. His favorite pastime was belting forth the *Exodus* song with contagious gusto. People of Kidapawan, North Cotabato bonded themselves together with him and the other "outreach religious" involved in social action programs in setting up organic farms and creating strong farmers cooperatives.

In 1974, Father Hagad was pastor of the Cathedral of Jolo. In February of that year Muslim rebels took the town. In the fierce fighting that followed when government forces came to recover Jolo from the rebels, the town was burned to the ground. Father Hagad, pastor of the Cathedral, was not hiding behind the remaining walls of his convento. He was in the midst of hundreds of terrified and confused Muslims and Christians running for their lives. Primo and a couple of Muslim leaders led them to safety towards Maubu. And, that sealed his warrant of arrest.

When things settled down and he was back at the Oblate residence, Primo was picked up by the military and brought to the stockade. He was questioned about his "highly irregular and unexpected association" with Muslim rebels and members of their families. The outcome of it all—damaged lungs, a broken eardrum, a broken rib—but not a broken heart. "It was during those months in the stockade," he said, "that I felt so close to God and to his people, and so I have made up my mind to devote my whole priestly life to the struggle of the people for social justice."

Proclamation through Notre Dame Schools. Very early in their ministry as Oblates in the Philippines, the priests realized the importance of molding the youth in the knowledge and love of Christ. To them, most of all, Jesus must be proclaimed in a clear, creative, and inspiring way. But how?

The answer came one day when a group of parishioners came to Father Beaudoin in Midsayap and they expressed the urgent need for a Catholic high school education for their children. The Oblates were not educators by any measure and schools were not part of the plan of "Oplan Cotabato" of Jolo. But then, Father Mongeau dared to move for a Catholic high school, if the people needed it. It was an opportunity for him, because a school was an effective way of teaching Jesus and the Gospel to students as they were being trained to acquire academic and practical skills for their life and future.

That first Notre Dame school in Midsayap, Cotabato [although it had to be closed because of the Second World War in December 1941] was opened in June 1941 with the help of the RVM Sisters. That was the mother-school of the chain of Notre Dame schools all over Cotabato, Sulu, and Tawi-Tawi—all in response to an urgent request of people whose lives the Oblates shared. Now, why Notre Dame? Mongeau's answer was: How fitting it is, Notre Dame, our lady. We have come here with Mary as our inspiration and guide. The Filipinos love the Blessed Mother so much and so they will love the name also. New co-workers also came who knew school-work; they came to the rescue—the Presentation Sisters and the Marist Brothers; they have good education and also have the ability to share Jesus with students, their parents and their teachers.

The fruitfulness of this venture is demonstrated by Notre Dame alumni in very responsible roles they maintain in government, schools, community service, and even in the Moro Islamic Liberation Front. Let me tell you a little story. One time in 1974 there was a fierce battle which erupted around the area of the Notre Dame University. There was the river and the rebels were on one side and the government troops were trying to assault them from the other side. Now in the lull between the fierce bursts of firing, people could clearly hear: *Mga sundalo, halina kayo, subukan n'yo ang mga Notre Dame boys!* That was our contribution to this struggle!

Notre Dame schools were sources of vocations to the priesthood and religious life among the Catholics, of course. But one unique distinction goes to Notre Dame of Sibutu, where a son of the local Muslim *imam* studied, heard about Jesus, watched the Fathers and other Christian preachers, saw the lives they led, and followed Him into the Church and into the holy priesthood—Fr. Busama Peter Nami, OMI.

The Notre Dame schools continue to proclaim and uphold gospel values to our Christian students and teachers. In the process, Muslims and others of various religious traditions hear about Jesus and see for themselves both the good and bad examples of the Christian way of life. The Notre Dame University in Cotabato City, led by Father Eliseo Mercado, OMI, is presently at the center of efforts for peace and reconciliation in Mindanao.

Mass Media. To bring Christ and Christian values to more and more people, the Oblates got into mass media; this was as early as 1947, years before *Inter Mirifica* of Vatican II. All began with the opening of the Notre Dame Press which printed Catholic instructional and devotional materials in the dialects. Weekly newspapers were also published; subsequently, the *Mindanao Cross* and the *Sulu Star* were published. Bishop Mongeau was not satisfied. When he became Bishop of Cotabato, the more he wanted to reach the last Christian person. It was that time he wrote the strong letter to Father Billman, who was in Manila; it seemed he was delaying in getting the franchise from the government. So, Mongeau wrote him: "You know that I think of radio, I speak of radio, I feel radio, and I dream radio; so, please get that franchise!" And so finally, DXMS, the first commercial, self-sustaining Catholic station in the country, began broadcasting in 1957. In subsequent years, other Oblate commercial stations began to make Christ and the Gospel values heard as far as the island of Sitangkai in Tawi-Tawi. All these, except the *Sulu Star*, as means of evangelization, continue to this day, in the words of *Inter Mirifica*, the Social Communication Decree of Vatican II, "to reach and influence, not only individuals but the very masses and the whole of society."

Personal and Communal Encounters with Christ. To provide people with a more personal, direct encounter with Christ and the proclamation of Jesus, the Cursillos of Christianity (1964) and the *Samaria*, its Ilonggo version (1967) were organized. These experiences gave a shot of religious fervor to about 15,000 men and women from all the parishes in Cotabato; it became a vital Oblate ministry.

Parish Ministry—Enriching the Faith of People. In the meantime, a deep awareness grew of our mission to proclaim a living faith in Jesus; it has to have deep and sturdy roots in the hearts of our people, the *masa*. This is the fruit of creative parish ministries which enkindled the faith of Catholics, especially through their experiences of the basic ecclesial communities (BECs) [GKKs in Cebuano]. Let me tell you a story about Sofronio Roxas—a Cebuano lay worker in the diocese of Kidapawan, North Cotabato. He was not directly involved in GKKs, but he worked with them and shared their aspirations.

There is a good number of lay people, men and women co-workers, whose example inspires the Churches of Mindanao. But, Sofronio Roxas was unique, for he sealed his testimony to the faith with his own blood. In 1983, with the leadership of the-then bishop of Kidapawan, Bishop Orlando Quevedo, OMI, Sofronio and other community leaders saw the people's helplessness in the face of military oppression and harassment, under the pretext of suppressing the onslaught of communism. So, people—mostly farmers—in *sitios* and *barangays* grovelled in fear of being arrested and accused of being communists. Sofronio Roxas, with a handful of other lay leaders, gathered them into a people's organization for mutual support, freedom from fear, and secure cooperative farming. They called it the "Lay Leaders Organization." Roxas was elected its first President. For this work of Christian leadership Sofronio was arrested several times by the military, but was released every time, for lack of any evidence of his having done anything against the law or morality.

In the midst of the threats against his life if he did not stop organizing farmers into strong communities of faith and life, he told his family, "*Ayaw kamo ug hilak sa akong kamatayon.* [Do not weep at my death.] It will be better if you continue what I have been doing. We are poor. This is our lot. We have to stay together in order to strengthen each other." To console and encourage his co-workers in the Church, he kept saying, to them, "*Ug ikaw adunay pagtoo* [if you have faith], you really have no problem anymore whatever happens to you. *Adunay Kristohanon nga pamaagi* [There is a Christian way of doing things]. This means that my work is not based on ideology. I'm doing my work, in his words, *pinasikad sa akong pagtoo.* My work is not to gain power but to fight for the good of the community [*alang sa kabulahanon sa katilingban*]."

On the morning of August 29, 1984, while riding his horse alone through a lonely sugarcane farm on the way home to his family, Sofronio Roxas was shot. He fell from his horse—dead on the spot, his blood drenching the soil that he and his co-workers worked so hard to make secure and productive for the people. That was the start of our work of proclaiming Jesus directly to our Christian Communities.

Proclamation To Muslim Communities. The experience of more than 60 years of living with Muslims shows that it is a losing proposition to proclaim Jesus our Savior directly by oral or written preaching. In the context of the revival of Islam, zealously orchestrated mostly by foreign fundamentalists and foreign-trained Filipino Islam teachers, the direct proclamation approach spells destructive and unproductive confrontation with leaders themselves.

Thus, the Oblates proclaim Jesus Christ by a life in which the face, the hands, the mind, and the heart of Jesus our Savior are perceived and appreciated by Muslims among whom they live and work as a community of His disciples. Let me recall Bishop Ben; Bishop Benjamin de Jesus, OMI, was the "Pied Piper" of Jolo. He went around the villages of the poor along the sea armed only with his big smile and a cheerful greeting for everyone he met. Children immediately ran up to him crying "Padel Ben! Padel Ben!" (which was their way of pronouncing "Father Ben"). You know, the people of Jolo never allowed him to be "Bishop Ben" (always "Father Ben").

More children would join this familiar procession when "Padel Ben" began to sing with them the *Baleleng*—the heart-song of Sulu and Tawi-Tawi. The Tausugs around in the alleys would greet him, make way for his singing procession, and the children cheered them on. And so, when he began singing, more children would come. This was the "crime" of Bishop Ben—to be with the poor, to side with them, to feel a big partiality for those who have nothing. And this, in the mind of certain rich and powerful people was against "their" law.

On February 4, 1997, Bishop Ben was felled with seven bullets, hitting him on the neck and chest at close range. Right there in front of his cathedral Bishop Ben de Jesus lay dead on the pavement. A few days before he died, he started wearing a black clerical shirt; when asked why, Bishop Ben calmly said to both Christians and Muslims, "I feel compassion for the people. They are suffering so much because of violence, oppression and murder, right here in our country. I mourn for Muslim and Christian victims of this situation." Bishop Ben had a dream—one human community, where Muslims, Christians and all, will live and work together in God's Name for justice, harmony, and peace. During the wake and the burial of Bishop Ben, there was no more distinction between Christians and Muslims. Everyone joined in the prayers, the talking, the conversations, the eating and drinking, the holding of hands during the *Our Father*. That was exactly what Bishop Ben was proclaiming to the Christians and witnessing to: that God is Father of all, that Jesus has come to bring us back to the Father. That was also what impressed Muslims: the way his life was lived, the way his words were spoken; they were all words of reconciliation, spoken for the unity and peace and brotherhood of all. So, brothers and sisters, as you can see, he was preaching directly to the Christian Community; he was also indirectly preaching to the Muslim Community.

Reflection. An experience can dispose a Christian to proclaim Jesus Christ the Redeemer of all peoples; one of these strong experiences is that of gratitude. It is a deep sense of gratitude for having been gifted with Christian Faith. By the power of God's Spirit, living faith generates such joyful gratitude in the human heart that it can impel that person to proclaim with zeal and creativeness Jesus the Savior—and the newness and richness which knowing Him brings.

I see this powerful sense of gratitude at the heart of the stories I have shared with you. As Oblates, we are inspired by the experience of our Founder, Saint Eugene de Mazenod. One day, he prayed to the crucifix in these words, "You have done so much for me.... What have I ever done for You?"

Here are also some inspiring and challenging words from *Ecclesia in Asia* (EA 10): "The Church's faith in Jesus is a gift received and a gift to be shared; it is the greatest gift that the Church can offer to Asia."

Mission And Inculturation

Pio Estepa, SVD

Some of you are perhaps familiar with the name of Fulton Sheen; he was a famous archbishop from New York, an eloquent speaker, and one of the Catholic pioneers of televised evangelization. He once said, "When your listeners applaud before your speech, it is an act of faith. If they applaud during your speech, it is an act of hope, and if they applaud afterwards it is an act of charity. I am very grateful for your applause of faith because among the list of speakers of this convention, I am the *incognito* in the Philippine Church. For 22 years ago, I was sent by you, our Philippine Church, on several missionary journeys: first in Africa, then in Latin America, and presently in Oceania. I could easily qualify for what Father Chito Tagle said yesterday, a "missionary tourist." Anyway, thank you very much for the invitation and for the warm welcome you are giving me.

Being given the task of a story teller, let me begin with a story. A middle-aged man went to a psychiatrist, and he said, "Doctor, I have a problem. My boss and my peers in the office, even my wife and my kids, are complaining, because they say I am very forgetful. I miss my appointments, I misplace things. My memory is failing me. Is there anything I can do about this problem?" The Doctor said, "Sir, since when have you been experiencing this problem?" The man said, "Problem? What's the problem?"

Life as Story. It surely is a problem, not only psychological but spiritual, when our memory starts to fail us, because our identity depends on our life story, on our memory; and, our life project depends on our identity. Our memory is very selective; what truly has an influence on our present, is not our past, but how we remember and interpret our past. Our memory selects a few experiences in the past and then combines them, weaves them into a life story, an autobiography. And, depending on whether we narrate our life story as a sad story or a tragedy or narrate it as a happy story or comedy, we narrow down or widen our hope for a better tomorrow. And so, if we ask, "Who am I?" "Who are you?" one meaningful answer is that each of us is a story. Some are interesting, others are boring, depending on how we interpret our life experiences and make our life story.

It is not just persons that are stories, but even peoples. My first mission appointment was in Zaire when it was still called Congo, and I worked as a bush pastor. I was working among a people that had very simple lives. At dawn, the men and the women together with the kids, the boys and the girls, would already start going from their huts in the bush toward the forest. The men are hunters and women are horticulturists. They practice a very primitive form of agriculture. They would come home only when the sun is going down. And so, during my first year there, I had to visit the villagers. The ones whom I encountered during the daytime in the villages were the pregnant women, the sick people, the babies and especially the grandparents, the elderly people. So a meaningful activity that I used to do was to befriend and listen to the stories of the old people, because there is a proverb in Africa which says: "the grandfather is a living library."

My experience though was that, when I started to ask them to share with me some of their proverbs, songs, and stories, they were very reluctant; often times, the reply that was given to me was, "Father, we have forgotten them. You see, with the coming of the Belgians, they said these are superstitions, these are products of ignorance. And so, being educated now and having become Christian, we really have forgotten them." But with time, as they came to accept me as a friend, little by little, they started sharing their stories. After four years, when my superiors had to call me back here to the Philippines, I had to say good-bye. And in the very simple farewell celebration that they gave me from village to village, I jokingly pointed a scolding finger to the grandparents in the community; I said, "You lied to me when I was a beginner here. You told me that you have no oral tradition anymore. But now, I am going back to my own Church enriched by your stories. Why did you lie to me?" One of the elderly catechists said, "You see, Father, the missionaries before you were just interested in sharing with us the story of Jesus, but they were not interested in the stories that come from our ancestors; they were branded as products of ignorance, of superstition, of paganism. But with you, it's different. You learned our language, you shared our life, you have become a friend of our villages, and so we want to share with you our stories so that you can understand us better."

So people are stories as well. And when we weave our past, it is never fixed. It is constantly changing as we reinterpret it, and as we reinterpret our past, we also renew our identity and constantly envision for ourselves a new life project.... By revising our life stories, we also renew our identity and project for ourselves a new vision as a person or as a people. If each of us is a story and if every people is a story, surely, it must have a theological consequence. Surely, it is inviting us to renew our understanding of evangelization and our understanding of inculturation.

Exploring Inculturation. This morning, what I would like to propose is not a new definition of inculturation but simply a narrative understanding of inculturation. Let me begin by offering a summary. I am sure it [my diagram] is not understandable immediately, but let this definition serve as the outline for the reflection that I will offer. A narrative understanding of inculturation is "the retelling of the Jesus story to a people or a generation in a way that it evokes enriching cultural *intertexts* from the collective mind and heart and offers them a meaningful life project for their present social contexts."

The first part is retelling the Jesus story. Evangelization and inculturation is retelling the Jesus story. If each of us is a story, if people are stories, even the Good News is a story. The theme of our Congress is written here, "Tell the World of His Love." Love is not a ritual. Love is not a doctrine. It is not even primarily an ethical norm or value. Love is first of all an experience, and if we say that love is an experience, therefore, it is the beginning of a relationship, a beginning of a story that constantly develops. The Bible then is not primarily a book containing rituals or a book of doctrines, not even a moral book. It is first of all, a story, a story of salvation. It is a story of how God relates to humanity in many saving ways. More than just a history of salvation, therefore, the Good News is a saving story.

In 1980-1981, I was sent to study in Paris, France in preparation for my mission to Zaire, Congo. It was the time when I got involved with organizing our many Filipinos and Filipinas working abroad; many came in at first as illegal workers. Afterwards, when I was sent to study in Rome, I also partly got involved in helping our chaplaincy centers to serve the needs of our Filipinos and Filipinas abroad.

Thanks to the generosity of the Catholic Bishops' Conference of the Philippines (CBCP), chaplaincy centers are multiplying today wherever many Filipinos can be found abroad. But optimistically, I think these chaplaincies are able to reach only fifteen percent of the many Filipinos working abroad. Some/many of them, I supposed, do not avail themselves of these chaplaincy centers, for the simple reason that they no longer find religion meaningful. I have talked to several of them and I ask them if they would like to join and participate in our activities. Their response is respectful, but a denial. They say, "Father, you see religion is no longer meaningful for me." Then, I ask them why.

Usually a very sad story follows: "You know I just come from a poor family in the Philippines and we had to sell our land or our property so that I can have money; we even had to borrow money from our relatives and friends. Then I fell into the hands of illegal recruiters or illegal travel agents. I was dumped somewhere in Eastern Europe. I had to struggle to sneak through the borders to reach Western Europe; now I find myself in a foreign land and I don't speak their language. I have had patrons/bosses who were very exploiting, but, you know, I managed without religion, without God. I don't need religion anymore." However, there are others who express a deepening of faith. I ask them what happened; what was your experience as a foreign Filipino worker? They would narrate the same sad experiences of getting indebted in the Philippines, of falling into the hands of illegal recruiters, passing through Eastern Europe to get into Western Europe and so on. But they said, "Every time, Father, we have always overcome, and so I experienced the provident hand of God, and I am grateful."

Two different types of people—with the same experiences; one group narrates a tragedy, another group a happy life adventure. Again, go back to what I said. It doesn't depend really on our past experiences but on how we interpret our past. Where a person plays God, he cannot encounter the presence of God in a life which is narrated as heroic tragedy; but, where we find a person who *lets God play* in his/her life and narrates an exciting adventure in that story, he/she discovers the presence of God. This is what evangelization or inculturation simply means. If we are stories, and the Gospel is a saving story, evangelization or inculturation consists of inter-weaving our life stories with the Jesus story in order to transform our human tragedies into what the poet Dante calls a "Divine Comedy."

Intertexts. The second part of the definition is that inculturation is retelling the Jesus story in a way that it evokes enriching cultural *intertexts* from their collective minds and hearts. Collective mind and heart is my definition of culture, but there is a neologism here that we encounter: the word *intertext*. It is a term I borrowed from the interpreters of symbols. It is a new term, but the idea actually is very old. We Filipinos, they say, are very fond of joking. And, we cannot joke without intertexts. I am sorry, but since I left the Philippines 22 years ago, I am not abreast with Erap jokes; when I left, it was Marcos jokes. And, *kahit na panis man ang joke na ito*, allow me to just give it as an example to explain the idea of intertext.

Remember in the late 1970s there was a booming business of instant photos and the company was called "Photo Me." Do you remember this? Does it still exist? Well, according to the joke, Bongbong, the son of the dictator bought that company, precisely because it was a very booming enterprise. And so, he renamed it from "Photo Me" to "Photo Bongbong." And then, because it caught the attention of his mother, Imelda also forcibly bought this company from him; so, she renamed the company from "Photo Bongbong" to *"Photo ng Ina ni Bongbong."*

The joke is possible only because of intertexts; a text that we hear, like "Photo Bongbong," recalls in our minds another text, which is a delicacy for us Filipinos which we eat at Christmas time, right? That other text of which we are reminded is what is meant by the word intertext. In the same way, when we say, *"Photo ng Ina ni Bongbong,"* we have a text—and I won't tell you what is the intertext. ˙

We can consider the Gospel message as a cultural text, i.e. text in the broad sense, not just something written but something that is proclaimed actively. And when we retell the Jesus story, in a new culture, for a new people, a new generation, it will always evoke other cultural intertexts from that culture.

Guadalupe. If you cannot grasp this idea, allow me to just give you an example from my experience in Latin America. You are very familiar with the picture of Our Lady of Guadalupe. Many of you would know the story and image of Guadalupe already. I will just stick to the graphic text of this image. To us who are Catholics, Christianized by Spaniards, it communicates easily; it is the image of our Blessed Virgin Mary. But, what about the Aztecs, the Nahuatls, the pre-Hispanic Mexicans?

In their Aztec mythology, the stars, the moon have meanings. The stars are children of a sky god and a sky goddesses. But then one day, like King David, the sky god was taking a walk on his balcony and looks down on earth and says, "Wow, she's beautiful, mother earth." And with her he had a relationship, and from her was born the sun. The sun is considered son of this illegitimate relationship between the sky god and the earth. Why? Because from the imagination, we see the sun come out from the earth at dawn and then go back to the earth at dusk. So they explained the phenomenon of night and day as a cosmic war. We remember that the Aztecs are a warrior people. There is an enmity between the sun against the stars and the moon. So when the stars and the moon are out there in the sky, the sun is not there. And when the sun is up there, the moon and the stars disappear. In this text they [Aztecs] would see a conflict between the rays of the sun behind her [the Virgin of Guadalupe] and the black moon at her feet.

In addition, the Virgin of Guadalupe wears pink clothing and on this pink clothing, we see patterns of flowers. Where do we find flowers? On earth. And so, for them it is the color of the earth. In contrast, we see her mantle is blue, and, patterned on the mantle of blue are the stars. Again—conflict. There are certain cultural symbols there which only an Aztec can understand. On her wrists are bracelets—symbols of virginity. A young girl would have to wear these up to the age of fifteen, until a young man proposes to her. But there is a conflict here, because she is wearing a black sash. In their culture, only a pregnant woman wears that as a sign of pregnancy.

This graphic conflict is resolved by this one image of a woman who is Aztec; she has an indigenous face, she looks like an Aztec. At the same time, her hands and fingers are very long; in Aztec culture this trait is associated with European women. In fact, studies of this image show us that there had been an attempt to shorten her fingers by painting over them, so that she would appear as totally an indigenous woman. Here then, we have the great image of a woman that is reconciling opposites, resolving conflict....

Here we have a graphic text which recalls two intertexts by contrast and by concord. And evangelization was mainly accomplished through this devotion to the Blessed Virgin Mary. For more than a hundred years, the ones who opposed this devotion were the Bishops and the Clergy. It was the lay people who promoted this devotion and evangelized Mexico....

I next proceed to explain the concept of *context* which is an easier concept. Context is another word for what biblical scholars would say, *sitz im leben*, a life situation, a social setting. When the Gospel is preached in a new social setting, it serves and unfolds "by comforting the afflicted and by afflicting the comfortable." It challenges, it questions, it invites toward a life project of repentance, conversion and renewal....

Conclusion. Going back to the definition that I gave you at the beginning, I hope it is now clear what I meant. **Inculturation** is re-telling the Jesus story to a people or a generation in a way that it evokes enriching cultural intertexts from their collective minds and hearts and offers them a meaningful life project from their present social context.

Let me sum up now my reflection by using an image. When a ray of white sunlight passes through a prison, that light refracts the richness of its colors. Similarly, when the Gospel message in all its purity passes through the prism of cultural diversity, it refracts a wealth of meaning. This passage is what I would call inculturation. And, I am very grateful to God for calling me to be an active witness of this process of refracting and refracting again the wealth of the Gospel message to different peoples—and as a representative of the Philippine Church! Thank you very much for your generous attention.

MISSION AND INTERRELIGIOUS DIALOGUE

A VIEW FROM BANGLADESH

Bob McCahill, MM

I want to begin by asking a question: "Who is the happiest person in the world that you know? Think for a minute: the happiest person in the world." Does anybody here think that he/she is the happiest person in the world? If you do, that is good, very good. I also think that I am the happiest person in the world. I don't see how anyone else could be happier. And, it is not the kind of happiness that is always laughing, always smiling. Rather, it is the happiness of **peace**, *kalinaw*. That happiness is mine, because I am privileged to work with the poor, to be useful to poor Muslims in Bangladesh. And, at the same time, I can be useful to the work of the Church in building trust, peace and harmony with people of other great faiths.

I have not always been this happy. When I was in college in Seattle University, I was making good grades in school; I was also making good money on a part-time job. That should have made me happy. But, in fact, I was miserable. Why? Because I did not know what was to be my future; I knew I had to do something good with my life, but I didn't know what it would be.

Then on October 31, 1956 (a long time ago), God showed me; God attracted me in a powerful way, a way so powerful that I could not ignore it: "Trust me. Give me everything. My love is enough for you." And so, I went to the seminary. I knew that the only way for me to be fulfilled was to be a priest and a missionary, to completely give myself to God. I went to the seminary, was ordained to the Priesthood in 1964, and was assigned to the Philippines. After language school in Sasa, Davao, I was assigned to Cateel, Davao Oriental, within the Tagum Prelature. Cateel was a beautiful place: the ocean, the mountains, the people. I came to love the Philippines. I was also assigned in other places in Davao Oriental (Mati, Caraga). Then I came back as pastor to Cateel. It was a wonderful time in my life. I was serving the people; I felt great fulfillment.

My feeling then as it is now was one of gratitude to God for calling me to be a priest and a missionary. If there is any charism that is given to me by God, it is the charism of gratitude. Later, I went to Zamboanga del Norte, to Sergio Osmeña Senior. Father Doug Venne was with me, and we went around the barrios, giving seminars. It was wonderful, satisfying work. I wanted to stay in the Philippines forever.

Then, an invitation came for volunteers to work in Bangladesh. I looked around; it seemed that the other people with me could very easily take over and carry on what we had begun together. So, I volunteered for Bangladesh. I thought that maybe I could do something there, maybe I could be of assistance to some people. Bangladesh had a very bad image at that time; it was an image of disaster. They had had a tidal wave in 1970 in which 300,000 people died; in 1971 they had a war in which at least a million died; in 1974 there was a famine in which at least 300,000 died. Floods every year; cyclones every year. I thought: "I'm a Christian, maybe I can do something there." I didn't know what I would do then, but I volunteered and went to Bangladesh.

Choosing an Apostolate. I would like to tell you about four people who helped me decide what I would ask the Archbishop of Dhaka to allow me to do. First, we had just arrived in Bangladesh and we were going by boat down the river. You know Bangladesh is a very riverine country. It is a country one-half the size of the Philippines, in which 130 million people live. On our first boat trip down the river, I saw a woman on the dock, probably 35 years old; she was obviously sick unto death. I attempted to speak to anybody to find out if someone could help her.

I finally found one gentleman who could speak English, and I asked him if there was something that could be done for the woman. He answered, "No." He wasn't being callous or cruel; he was simply being, he thought, realistic. There are many people like this woman and there is no way that we can help them, no way we can help them all. When I got back on the boat I said in my mind "Yes, there is something that should be done and maybe I can do something, after I finish language school."

Although language school finished, we were not yet able to decide on our commitment, what we would do in Bangladesh. The Archbishop was giving us time in order to look around. So, I went to see a priest, a very respected, elderly priest in Calcutta in West Bengal (India). I went to see Father Celestine, and I asked him about his experience. Father told me a very important fact. He said that when he came to the country the purpose of working among Muslims was to convert them. He was involved in college and youth hostel work. In this context he tried to convert the Muslims. And, for ten years he spoke to Muslim students to attract them to the Christian faith; none of them showed any interest.

One day Father Celestine was on the street with a Muslim boy, who he had been trying to lead to the Christian faith. While they were talking, they noticed a man in the gutter nearby. After some time, two women in white saris came along and went to the man in the gutter, consoled him, gave him some water to drink, and lifted him out of the gutter. When Father Celestine glanced at the Muslim boy, he saw tears running down his cheeks. He was moved. Probably, that boy never became a Christian, but certainly at that moment he understood Allah, the merciful and compassionate one, better than ever before. Father Celetine's contribution to my choice of apostolate had been made.

The next person who led me to decide what to do in Bangladesh was Mahatma Gandhi—that great man from India. He loved Jesus and had great respect for missioners and for what they were trying to do. Mahatma Gandhi was thrilled by reading the Sermon on the Mount; he thought that it was among the most beautiful scriptures that he had ever read. Gandhi saw that in India the missionaries were working to convert people. In effect, he believed that the approach was wrong—for these people in this place.

Gandhi advised: "Be like the rose. A rose is beautiful just by looking at it. You should try to live among us as servants—simply." He said all this in a very memorable quote: "A life of service and of uttermost simplicity is the best preaching"— to his people at that time and in that place. I say that a life of dedicated service to the poor is the most authentic preaching. Gandhi said these things in a book, ironically entitled: *The Message of Jesus Christ.* So, I assume ways of simplicity.

The fourth person who taught me what to do in Bangladesh, who taught me how different the people from Bangladesh are in attitude from those here in the Philippines, was Habib, a young man from the first town in which I lived. Habib said: "Remember, for us Bengali Muslims, there is **no** disinterested person; we do not believe in unselfishness, in altruism. We do not believe that anyone does good simply because it is good to do it. We believe that everybody has an angle. For example, if someone wants to give you education, it is really to get you into his religion. We feel there is no disinterested person."

Based on all this input and with the permission of the Archbishop, ultimately, we five Maryknollers decided to go to the Muslims, to do service, and to do it simply. We wanted to be good samaritans, to be among the people as brothers. Where there is suspicion, let us sow trust.

Daily Life. Now, what I presently do and what I have done for the past twenty-five years is to go around by bicycle, looking for people who need very much to go to hospitals. I take them or I invite them. Some go, some say they will go and do not go, and others refuse outright. I try to help people, as Gandhi recommended. I really try to be "downwardly mobile." I try to live with the people as much as possible. I have a bamboo hut in a Muslim neighborhood. I draw my own tube-well water; I bathe in the public pond where everyone else bathes. I go to the public market everyday to buy fresh vegetables, because there is no refrigeration. And, I simply try to live as "brother" to them.

People ask me "What are you doing here? Who are You?" I simply tell them: "I am your brother, Bob." There are no Christians in the town. They ask me: "What do you do?" I tell them: "I do what Jesus did. Because Jesus went around doing good and healing people, I try to follow him." Jesus didn't have a bicycle, but he went around. People were attracted to Jesus by his curing and especially by his compassion. He had compassion for people.

Bengali Muslims are just like the people of Galilee; they are attracted by compassion. I'm often asked: "What profit is there for you in this work? How many dollars do you get for taking each person to the hospital?" I try to explain to them that the only "profit" that I make is blessing from God. I'm content with the blessing of God. I'm trying to show them that unselfishness is the heart of Christianity. Service to the stranger is the kind of love that the Good Samaritan showed.

The Bengali people that I am privileged to work with now have several characteristics that you would be interested in. They are handsome, good-looking people. They are a poetic people; I never met so many young people whose ambition is to be a poet. And, they are curious people, always asking questions, direct questions also. After they ask you what you are doing and what is your profit, they may directly ask you how you control your sex and where you get your money. There is no obstacle to asking questions.

I spend three years in each town. For the first year, the people are suspicious of me. I try to break down the suspicions. I try to take their people to the hospital or where they would like to go, need to go, and thus, break down suspicions. Many will not go, because they do not trust the foreign Christian. By the second year trust is established with many people. And they see that I have no reason for helping them except the love of God and that they need to be helped. I can help; therefore, I do help. This second year of trust-building is proven when the men allow me to take their wives, daughters, sisters and mothers to the hospital.

In the third and final year, I can see that some people actually like me and have affection for me. They see that I am concerned for them and that I have a heart for them. Therefore, they have affection, and I thank God for that.

Encouragement and Support. Bishop Francis A. Gomes of Mymensingh Diocese, with I whom am working now, writes a letter for me every time I go to a new town. I stay three years in a town and go to another town, towns that are apart by sixty or one hundred miles. I have to have this letter in case the police come and ask: "What are you doing here?"

In his letter the bishop says: "Live among the poor as a brother to them." We are their brothers; we believe that they are our brothers. God is one, and God's family is one. This is new to Muslims. In other words, the Muslim, Hindu, Buddhist, Christian—all are God's family.

The second point the bishop gives to me is: "Serve the sick so that they may live." In other words, I'm there because we want the Muslim Bengalis to continue living; we value their lives. The third point of the bishop is: "Show the respect that we have for Muslims and Hindus. Demonstrate the respect of Catholic Christianity for Islam and Hinduism." I have occasion to praise them for their prayers done regularly, because they are exemplary, many of them, at prayer. I also praise them for giving alms even when they have very little for themselves. I praise them for going on pilgrimage—local and to Mecca. And finally, I praise them for their fasting—and I join them. We can join them in their fasting, and they will not think that we have become Muslims because they know we are Christians and fasting is a Christian custom; we can do it with them.

Inspiring Companions.   I would now like to tell you about of some of my Bengali companions; they are excellent companions on our way to God. Lal Banu is a woman who begs for a living because she is blind. She is 25 years old; she sits along the path in the village. She does nothing else but beg. She has no husband; she is very friendly. Her only survival comes from what she gets from begging. When I went past one day, Lal Banu raised her sari and said, "Look, it has holes in it. Will you get me a sari?" And I said, "Lal Banu, your sari has holes in it and it is very hot today. You have an air-conditioned sari." And she was so merry; she was so tickled by that. Think of it: this woman has nothing in the world except what's in that little plastic bag she keeps—and she is always ready to laugh. She is not at all defeated by blindness and aloneness....

Another companion on my way to God is Renu. She is a slight, dark, pretty sixteen-year-old girl and has cirrhosis of the liver. She was pleased whenever I would visit and gently slap my baseball cap on her head. One day I found her in pain, lying outdoors with an old umbrella shading her rapidly aging face. "I've never had a sari of my own," the dying lass declared. Would you rather have additional medicine or a sari? I asked. "A sari!" she shot back. "A pink sari," she added with a smile. After I had been to ten sari shops, I found an entirely pink one. Renu got up from her mat and let women drape her with her first sari. I took some photos; she posed good-naturedly. Renu accepted that she would die within 15-20 days. Frailty is no obstacle to bravery. Weakness is no obstacle to courage. How often I see this! I am inspired!

My daily schedule starts at 4:00 a.m. I get up and have a cup of coffee. Then, I pray for an hour in the dark, since there is no electricity. I just tell God what I've been telling God for the past 40 years: "I love you, I thank you." After that, I celebrate mass; I finish by six o'clock. Then I have breakfast. By seven o'clock I get on the bicycle and go out for six hours. Perhaps I've been told that in some village there is a person who needs to see me. Maybe the village is 5-10 kilometers away, the further the better—because it allows more people to see me on the road. They will ask questions: "Who is he? What is he doing here?" And, people begin to talk. They often have many stories, correct and incorrect.

Some think I'm a reporter, a spy, a policeman (no compliment), a doctor. A few will say I'm a missionary—which is *not* a compliment in a country that has had a colonial history; a missionary is part of the government apparatus that came to conquer them and subdue them. And so, they don't like missionaries. Thus, when they ask me who I am, I tell them: "I'm your brother, Bob; I am a Christian, Catholic missionary." I want them to hear that, because their idea of a missionary is from a time that has passed. I don't come to conquer you; I come, because Christ has conquered me. I come to you in love as a brother. They accept that, and it is the poor who accept the offer of brotherhood and friendship almost immediately….

A biscuit—the lowly biscuit—is a very great treasure in the hand of a Bengali child. There are no cupboards in most Bengali houses, so when you break open a bag of biscuits, eat them quickly! One time I was visiting a village and Alameen, a child 2-3 years-old who had osteomyelitis in his shoulder was in his mother's arms. I was speaking to the mother and then Alameen took his biscuit and slowly held it out to me. He wasn't sure whether I was friend or foe, but after I spoke to his mother, he was sure I was a friend. He gave me his biscuit. I put out my hand to test him, and he put it in my hand. You might think that it is not a very expensive thing. It is wealth for a Bengali child. He gave it away. Children in Bangladesh, Muslim children, learn early in life to share.

Adults share also. One day I went to the house of Jabeda, a woman to whom I had given worms medicine two months earlier; it is very inexpensive medicine. When Toyob Uddin, her husband, saw me, he told his oldest daughter to go get the stool from his neighbor's house and bring it so I could sit down. The other daughter went inside and got their only dish. The mother came out of the mud house and brought out two mangoes. They had them in the house so they could take them to the market and sell them. But they cut up the mangoes and insisted that I eat them. The mangoes cost more than the worm medicine that I gave them. And these people had nothing else. Poverty is no obstacle to generosity. Destitution is no obstacle to unselfishness. They inspire me!

Walking Together. One time when I moved to a new town, after I'd been there several months, a family invited me to come and build a house in their property. And so, I went. Nazim Uddin and his wife Golenor would help me build the house. It takes three days to put up a bamboo hut. They were doing the skilled labor and I was the *dodong* there. I was digging the holes with my hands for the posts. At one moment Nazim Uddin and I were taking a break, but

Golenor continued working. She was pulling potatoes out of the ground so that the potatoes would not come up through my floor. And she sang out as she worked; she said, "See how people here hold you in *mahabot* (Allah's love). While you are with us, you will never lose anything." What a wonderful thing to hear in Bangladesh, where there's much petty theft. I hear this woman who lives in a wrecked hut pledge that she'll protect my hut, the bicycle I keep in it, and the clothes I put on the line while I am not at home. That's wonderful. She's got her priorities straight. She'll watch my stuff rather than improve her own home, rather than work on decorating her own poor place.

One of my heroes is Belayet, a man about forty, uneducated. I took him to the hospital, admitted him, and the next week when I went back, Belayet was finished. The doctor did not want to keep him anymore. And so as I'm bringing him downstairs, holding him up, he said, "I couldn't eat all week long." And I said, the only thing I could say, the only true thing I could say to him was: "Belayet, Allah loves you. Belayet, Allah knows what you are going through. Belayet, you are a good man." A couple of weeks later, Belayet was no more. I fully expect that the one thing I said to him that stuck in his mind was the one thing that people do not say to ragged, dirty, uneducated, unsandalled, "un-everything" people; that was: "Belayet, you are good." He suffered. If I didn't see the suffering of Jesus Christ in people like Belayet, I would be a blind man.

One other example is Elim. Every Friday I have the custom of taking a Muslim to a meal. I go to the bazaar, then after the Islamic prayer, when they are coming out of the mosque and if I see somebody who looks particularly in need of a meal, I invite him to have some curry. Elim came with me to a restaurant and had a plate of curry and rice [Bengalis love fish curry, very hot stuff]; at the end of the meal he gave thanks. I was a footnote in his prayer. He prayed and praised Allah—for having given the food, for having given the place to eat, the appetite, the whole works. He mentioned me, but his thanks was to Almighty God. I think that you and I would agree that his priorities are correct. God is to be thanked for every gift we get—God first, last and always. Nobody is more worthy of our gratitude than the God we serve.

I would like to close with a brief word, a saying that one of my companions in Bangladesh (Doug Venne) frequently quotes; it is valid for all of us. The quote comes from Charles de Foucauld: "Shout the Gospel with your lives." It's the loudest instrument we have!

MISSION AND INTERRELIGIOUS DIALOGUE WITHIN INTEGRAL EVANGELIZATION

James H. Kroeger, MM

This presentation is intended to be an overview of the Church's current thinking regarding the role of dialogue in the mission of the Church; it is also designed to complement the actual experience of dialogue. We have been privileged to hear many beautiful and inspiring *experiences of living dialogue*, as they were creatively narrated by Bob McCahill employing his rich Bangladesh experience. The stories Bob told and the people he introduced to us are inspiring and enriching. They come from a faith-filled missionary, and, as Bob said in the beginning, from a very happy missionary. My task is to complement those stories with some *theological-missiological reflection*; appreciate my input in conjunction with what Bob has said. I will present some ideas on the vision of dialogue and how dialogue is integrated within the mission of the Church.

Some basic questions to be asked are: Why do we engage in dialogue? How is this part of the Church's total mission of evangelization? The first point I would like to make is this: since the time of the Second Vatican Council (1962-1965) and *Evangelii Nuntiandi* (1975), the understanding of mission in the consciousness of the Church has expanded and grown. Mission and evangelization are to be comprehended—and accomplished—in a comprehensive, total, integral way. Pope Paul VI has said that evangelization today "means bringing the Good News into all strata of humanity" (EN 18). This means that evangelization is necessarily a very rich endeavor and process.

In this National Mission Congress we are hearing about evangelization understood as inculturation, proclamation, as interreligious dialogue and human promotion. There are presentations on mission theology and spirituality. Twenty different specialized workshops explore various aspects of mission today. Yes, evangelization has a wonderful richness and complexity! And, as the apostolic nuncio noted in his homily last evening, the Church now looks at this entire process as "integral evangelization." The Second Plenary Council of the Philippines in 1991 committed the entire Philippine local Church to "a renewed integral evangelization" (Part III, 154-401).

The several elements of evangelization all reinforce and complement each other. It is not a matter of always starting at one point and following an orderly pattern; diverse situations and contexts require different approaches and emphases. The commonly understood elements of "integral evangelization" are: **(A)** Witness of Christian Life; **(B)** Service of Humanity; **(C)** Interreligious Dialogue and Inculturation; **(D)** Explicit Gospel Proclamation; and, **(E)** Prayer, Contemplation, Liturgy and Sacraments. A brief word on each element is necessary; a more elaborate discussion on interreligious dialogue will follow.

A. According to Pope Paul VI, the **witness of our lives** as Christians is the "initial act of evangelization" (EN 21). All our daily activities, living together in harmony, our lives as individuals and families, our duties in our communities: all these are to be a basic "faith-witness" that our values and lives are shaped by our Christian belief. Through this wordless witness, "Christians stir up irresistible questions in the hearts of those who see how they live" (EN 21). And, in today's world, people will listen "more willingly to witnesses than to teachers"; people will listen precisely to Christians when "they are witnesses" (EN 41).

B. Our common living should naturally issue in **our service of humanity.** This means serving the most unfortunate, witnessing to justice, defending the integrity of creation; it includes the whole area of social concerns, ranging from peace-building, education and health services, to promoting family life and good government. The area of human development or human promotion is a vast field for Christian mission.

C. Here in Asia these activities naturally assume an interreligious context and manifestation. The Church in Asia accomplishes her mission in pluralistic societies and diverse cultures; she enters into **interreligious dialogue**, cooperating with the followers of the great religious traditions, so pervasive in all Asian countries. "Christian" Philippines is also home to Muslims, Buddhists, and local religions.

D. In mission there is the role of **explicit Gospel proclamation.** This element of evangelization includes preaching, catechesis on Christian life, teaching the content of the faith; in a word, this means "telling the Jesus story." When the Holy Spirit opens the door and when the time is opportune, we do tell the Jesus story, we do give explicit witness and testimony to our faith. We invite others, in freedom of conscience, to follow, to come to know Jesus. By proclamation we are both instructed in the Christian faith and communicate that faith to the next generation of believers.

E. The final dimension of integral evangelization centers on **prayer, contemplation, liturgy and sacraments.** No one can effectively be in mission without a strong prayer-life. Both individually and communally, we live and celebrate our faith. Our reflection and prayer illumine all dimensions of mission.

Obviously, these five dimensions of an integral understanding of evangelization complement and reinforce each other. Much more could be said about each of these elements. Be aware that the vision of integral evangelization is a composite overview of mission today; it is also at the heart of the structure of our National Mission Congress.

Church: Community-in-Dialogue. Turning to the specific area of interreligious dialogue, we return to core questions: Why does the Church engage in dialogue? Why is dialogue the preferred and accepted mode of mission in Asia today? The Asian Church leadership, the Federation of Asian Bishops' Conferences (FABC), has strongly encouraged the approach of dialogue. For example, when speaking of Muslim-Christian relations, the FABC has stated: "Christians living among Muslims should recognize the importance of dialogue with their Muslim brethren. For most Christians this means what can be called a dialogue of life. This is the most essential aspect of dialogue.... We encourage Christians to be ever more deeply involved in this dialogue of life" (BIRA II, 14). This can all be summarized in three words: "Be Good Neighbors." Dialogue is all about "good neighbor-ology."

This dialogue of life is much more than simply humanitarian concern or working together in social development projects. In these common activities we are engaged in a profound endeavor; Pope Paul VI termed this activity "the dialogue of salvation" (*Ecclesiam Suam* 75-79). Because they are common pilgrims on the way to God, Muslims, Hindus, Buddhists, Christians inspire each other; they encourage each other on the path toward God and holiness. As people of faith, Christians do this because we truly believe that the Holy Spirit is present and assists us. Together we are moving along the path of salvation.

Interreligious dialogue, therefore, is not only some external activity. Obviously, we do not lose or sacrifice our faith in dialogue; in fact, authentic dialogue strengthens faith. We can appreciate more deeply what the Second Vatican Council and Pope John Paul II have consistently emphasized; they assert that being "linked with the paschal mystery...holds true not only for Christians, but for all people of good will in whose hearts grace works in an unseen way.... [Christians] ought to believe that the Holy Spirit in a manner known to God offers every person the possibility of being associated with this paschal mystery" (*Gaudium et Spes 22; Redemptoris Missio 6, 10, 28*).

God's grace continually works in unseen ways. We are called to believe in the marvelous action of the Holy Spirit. I find this very profound. It was said 35 years ago in the Vatican Council. It was reiterated very strongly by our Holy Father in his mission encyclical. Did you know that in the very long mission encyclical, *Redemptoris Missio*, there is only *one* quote from all of scripture and Vatican II that is used more than once? The quote is this one which so strongly affirms the action of the Holy Spirit in the lives of all people. Think about it; I find this reflection of John Paul II startling. This is certainly a pivotal emphasis in the mission theology of the pope.

Additional Signposts. There are three or four other guideposts for dialogue that I would like to share with you. I choose them because they inspire me and help set the direction in which we should be moving. Again, Vatican II in its document on Non-Christian Religions said: "The Church has this exhortation for her members: prudently and lovingly, through dialogue and collaboration with the followers of other religions, and in witness of the Christian faith and life, acknowledge, preserve, and promote the spiritual and moral goods found among these people, as well as the values in their society and culture" (*Nostra Aetate* 21). Again, it goes without saying, I think that a vivid example of this guideline put into action can be found in the way Brother Bob goes about mission among his Muslim neighbors in Bangladesh.

Another guidepost can be found in John Paul II's mission encyclical: "Interreligious dialogue is part of the Church's evangelizing mission.... The Church sees no conflict between proclaiming Christ and engaging in interreligious dialogue.... Each member of the faithful and all Christian communities are called to practice dialogue" (RM 55/57). Dialogue is not an after-thought, something you do after you finish everything else. It is part of the Church's evangelizing mission. There is *no conflict* between proclaiming Christ and engaging in interreligious dialogue. The next line is addressed to all of us: "Each member of the faithful and all Christian communities are called to practice dialogue." We all have to find concrete paths to engage in dialogue.

John Paul II in his many missionary journeys around the world always requests that he has an opportunity to meet with non-Christians. He made a very symbolic and significant act in 1986 when he called the followers of the world's great religions, large and small, to come together in Assisi, the home of St. Francis. This is what he said in his opening greeting: "I have the honor and pleasure of welcoming all of you for our World Day of Prayer in this town of Assisi.... The very fact that we have come to Assisi from various quarters of the world is in itself a sign of the common path which humanity is called to tread.... Either we learn to walk together in peace and harmony, or we drift apart and ruin ourselves and others." Our Mindanao experience has proven this statement; we are learning to walk together; we also have often ruined peace and harmony.

The final signpost that I would offer is something that John Paul II said on his missionary journey in Manila on February 21, 1981: "Christians will, moreover, join hands with all men and women of good will [and] work together to bring about a more just and peaceful society in which the poor will be the first to be served." In other words, a clear endeavor of dialogue is to come together—Muslims, Christians, Buddhists—so that in unity we may serve the needy.

Many additional dialogue insights are available. I recommend you search the book *Tell the World* for several wonderful Filipino examples of interreligious dialogue; I know you will appreciate the lives and work of Bishops Bienvenido Tudtud and Benjamin de Jesus, OMI. Friends, we have explored the **theology** of dialogue; the **daily practice** of dialogue is even more urgent and important!

Mission and Human Promotion

Louie G. Hechanova, CSsR

Introduction. My story is about an incident that happened to me 30 years ago. I was giving a mission in a remote rural barrio in Sibalom Parish, Province of Antique. Because of poverty, many people from Antique go over to Negros Occidental during the milling season as *sacadas* or migratory workers to help cut sugarcane and thus augment their income. This particular night, the mission activities were over and the people had shared with me the little food that they had. As was my practice, I lingered awhile chatting with the people. It was then that a woman asked me a question that jolted me: "*Padre, may Dios bala ang kalibutan?*" Is there a god in the world?

Now wait a minute, I said to myself. Where is this question coming from? Can it be coming from Atheism? Have some Marxists penetrated this barrio and sown doubts about God's existence among these people? A few questions to the woman convinced me that this was not the case. Rather it was coming out of their situation of poverty. Her question was not so much about the existence of God, but about God's goodness. It could be paraphrased in this way: "Since God exists and he is supposed to be a good, loving Father, how come He has left us in this situation?" In other words, she was trying to reconcile her faith in God with her situation of poverty which seemed to contradict it. And she was expressing a belief, a conviction that somehow salvation cannot be all spiritual, but must also affect the other dimensions of her life, including the socio-economic. In other words, she believed in human life. She made me realize that for people like her poverty is not merely a sociological problem, it poses a question about God. It is a theological problem.

Mission and Human Promotion. The topic given to me uses the phrase "human promotion," a term more commonly used in Europe for what we call "human development." I don't want to enter into a discussion regarding which term is more preferable, human development or human promotion. In the final analysis both mean the same thing. I would rather put the emphasis on what is common between them which is the word "human." In other words, we are being asked to reflect on what the Mission of Christ has to do with human beings and what is human in this world. In fact, the full title carries the suggestion that Christ's mission is geared towards human promotion, the fulfillment of God's plan for the human family and the full development of the human potential in life. The 1971 Synod of Bishops says: "Action on behalf of justice and participation in the transformation of the world appear to us as a constitutive dimension of the preaching of the gospel, or in other words of the Church's mission for the redemption of the human race and its liberation from every oppressive situation" (*Justice in the World*, Introduction). So these two aspects are not to be separated.

This point has become very important in today's world. Why do the Jews blame Pope Pius XII who is not their own church leader for not publicly condemning Nazism, which eventually exterminated some six million Jews? Because of their perception—the way they read history—they think that he sacrificed a problem of humanity in favor of a parochial concern to avoid Church persecution. On the other hand, why were the Jews so moved by the present Pope's recent visit to the Holy Land despite his refusal to blame Pope Pius XII as some of them expected? Because he was perceived to be genuinely sympathetic to their sufferings and had humbly said sorry and apologized for what Christians had done to Jews and others in past history. What this says to us is that the Church is more admired when it acts humbly and courageously on that which touches and promotes the good of humanity than when it acts merely for its own parochial concerns as a Church. Closer to home, this was one great merit of Cardinal Sin's action during EDSA. He risked the institutional interests of Radio Veritas in favor of the Kingdom values of truth, justice, freedom, love and peace. Yes, the transmitter of Radio Veritas got destroyed in the process, but the Misereor people I talked to in Europe told me how proud they were to see that Radio Veritas played the role they had always hoped for and that they were only too happy to replace every nut and bolt that was destroyed. Radio Veritas had played at last a prophetic role in society and did not just remain or degenerate into a pious radio station playing music all day when all the injustices were happening all around us.

Human Promotion in the Asian Context. *Ecclesia in Asia*, the Synod document promulgated by Pope John Paul II, strongly emphasizes that Jesus is Asian by birth and that it was in Asia that the gospel was first preached. But it is also quick to point out the puzzling fact that He is so little known in this continent. With more than 60 percent of the world population, Asia is less than 3% Christian in population. At the same time, it expresses the hope that this new millenium will see an increase of Christians in this part of the world through the explicit proclamation of the uniqueness of Christ's salvation. However, in the same document, one can also read all sorts of caution coming from the Asian Church people who spoke up at the Synod that this missionary undertaking is not as simple as it might appear. The cultural pitfalls are many since the major religions of the world are the cultural religions of many Asian countries. An aggressive evangelism in the style of Protestant fundamentalists [like Wilde Almeda's] could well provoke a backlash and become counterproductive. Indeed, in a continent that takes religion so seriously, holy wars are a constant danger [note what is going on in Maluku, Indonesia, and the Jihad declared by the MILF].

One of the most effective ways of interreligious dialogue, as advocated by FABC, is a dialogue of life. And one of the best ways of engaging in a dialogue of life is human promotion through the social ministry provided that it does not carry any tinge of proselytism. On the ground, many Asians of other faiths are generally suspicious of Christians (Catholic and especially Protestant) when they engage in social work. They think it is all a gimmick of conversion. But, when Christians sincerely reach out to the poor, the needy, the victims of disasters or human rights violations, etc. and can prove that they have no ulterior proselytizing motives, a true dialogue of life can take place. Example: when a Muslim family lost their home in a fire in Davao City, Father Paul Cunanan asked his mother to take them into their home. This Muslim family lived with them for three months. And this dialogue of life has gone a long way to promote good relations between Muslims and Christians in Davao.

Besides, in places in Asia where communist governments are still in power, the only way for the Church to find a role is in the field of human promotion.... It is the same in China. Until now, priests and religious are generally not welcomed to China for purely pastoral or missionary work. But if they teach English, the government allows them to come in incognito. You can be sure someone in the government knows they are priests and religious missionaries, but they are tolerated for the social service they render. The Benedictine Sisters of Tutzing have been invited to open a hospital in China and they are now with a community of eight and ready to open it as soon as some administrative problems are ironed out with the government authorities.

Human Promotion in the Philippine Context. The Spaniards who came to the Philippines in the 16th century had no problem linking the Christian mission with human promotion. Faith and civilization were the two goals they set out to share with the Indios wherever they would meet them. Unfortunately, most of the friars could not distance themselves from their patrons and therefore could not sympathize with the Filipinos' aspiration for political freedom. As a result they suffered the same fate with Spanish colonialism during the revolution and some 700 of them had to leave the country and go home to Spain.

It was with the separation between Church and State, introduced during the American colonial period, that the link between Mission and Human Promotion was weakened for a while. For this separation tended to compartmentalize human life into temporal and eternal, material and spiritual and tried a division of labor that assigned the temporal to the State and the spiritual to the Church. But this exaggerated compartmentalization could not be sustained for too long. Inevitably, one sphere encroached on the other and mutual charges of interference were the order of the day. Wasn't the Church interfering in the temporal sphere when Father Hogan SJ promoted the organization of a labor union (FFW), whatever its claim to be Christian inspired? Wasn't the State going beyond its proper sphere when it prescribed Rizal's books, condemned by the Church for being anti-clerical, as acquired reading in schools?

These questions were to grow more critical during the Martial Law period. Could the Church remain unmoved in the face of the grinding poverty of the people and not try to promote some socio-economic self-help projects, cooperatives and community development programs? Love of God, after all, demanded the horizontal dimension of love of neighbor. And St. James asks what is the use of that which does not show itself in deeds? If a person came to you with his need and you just tell him "good luck" and sent him home empty-handed, how can you claim that you love God? On the other hand, the government was asking: aren't the Basic Christian Communities (BCCs) in Mindanao subversive organizations whose leaders should be arrested? Human rights, justice, peace, truth, and freedom: to whose proper sphere do they belong? In the context of Martial Law it was inevitable for a prophetic Church and a repressive State to find themselves on a collision course.

It was the EDSA event of 1986 that settled the whole matter. After 14 years of Martial Law, it had gradually become clear that involvement was not only in economics, but also in politics. These are moral issues in which the Church had a right and duty both to announce prophetically God's judgment, as well as denounce situations contrary to it as the prophets did in the Old Testament. EDSA was our bishops' finest hour during the whole period of Martial Law; they questioned the moral basis for Marcos to continue to rule based on an election marked by unprecedented fraudulence.

In the aftermath of EDSA, the Church proclaimed itself a Church of the Poor at PCP-II, "a Church that lives in evangelical poverty which combines detachment from material possessions with a profound trust in the Lord as the only source of salvation; a Church that defends and vindicates the rights of the poor even when doing so spells for itself alienation or persecution; a Church where the poor, equal to all others in Christian dignity, are not only evangelized but become evangelizers themselves; a Church where no one is so poor as to have nothing to give, and no one is so rich as to have nothing to receive." Ten years later I hear that the Bishops are preparing to evaluate how well PCP-II has been implemented. At least one archbishop told me that it was flawed for not having adequate structures for implementing its beautiful decrees. And we are now in the post-EDSA era where the Church's mission for human promotion is more relevant than ever, but where a number of equations have changed.

In the economic sphere, no one any longer questions whether Church people have a role in promoting livelihood projects for the poor, cooperatives and community development. The question is the more subtle one of how much control they should maintain over such projects and how much autonomy to give to the people concerned. Must Church people always be in the forefront, *palaging bida,* in promoting projects or can they be catalysts in the background who know how to promote effective people's participation in their own projects? Can we be satisfied with being mere support groups to peoples' organizations?

... In the sphere of public life in this post-EDSA period, Church people are seen to be not only taking part in mass actions but even leading them, e.g. the anti-Cha-Cha rallies during the Ramos administration and the anti-Concord rallies during this present administration. In the glow of the initial popularity he enjoyed early in his administration, President Estrada used to play down the opinion of Church people believing himself more in tune with the true feelings of the *masa.* The drastic drop in his popularity rating due in part to the Concord issue, has sobered him up and he has begun to listen once again to advice from some Church people. The populist nature of his leadership style deserves careful monitoring and close-guarding....

The fact that as Church people we have shown ourselves capable of galvanizing public opinion around certain issues and able to influence public policy carries a weighty responsibility and challenge. While we seem to be good at taking the pulse of the people, it can also happen that at times we are not sufficiently conversant and well informed regarding some of the issues we take up. There is a tendency among us to be too idealistic and lacking some of the pragmatism that at times is the only way to resolve certain issues. On the other hand, some Church people can also show that they do have the facts because they are close to the people, know how to do research and have bothered to do their homework. This suggests that we could be more judicious in the choice of issues to comment on. We could avoid being too trigger happy shooting from the hip on any and all issues that arise. If we kept to issues that have a fairly clear moral dimension, we could maintain a high credibility rating before the public. We could work out ways of collaborating with other forces in Civil Society in doing advocacy work, lending our influence but without seeking to dominate.

The culture of corruption has been endemic in our country in all administrations since independence and does not give a good image to our Christian society before our Asian neighbors. Unfortunately, most of our religious movements are geared towards the conversion of individuals who have to go back into the same environment of corruption. What we need is a religious movement led by concerned lay people that would help reform an entire office or work group in such a way that honesty and transparency become the normal practice in their work environment and where there is a mechanism for enforcing these practices or penalizing violators.

The perceived drift and ineptitude of the present administration provides the Church a particular challenge as a catalyst for change in our society at the present time. In playing this role, I think there are two temptations to be avoided. The first is to fall into what I call the "Manalo Syndrome," the temptation to develop a "Catholic vote" in the style of the *Iglesia ni Cristo* with Church people openly endorsing or campaigning for particular political candidates. In isolated cases this might be effective, but over the long haul it could mean disaster for the Church. The second temptation is to use our social influence to enhance the privileges and institutional interests of the Church rather than the true social welfare of the people. *Mag-ingat tayo*, lest we lose the respect of our own people who will brand us as *mukhang pera* or *matapobre*.

In this connection, it is good to laud the approach that many of our Church leaders are taking regarding the Mindanao conflict. We have experienced Church persecution in Basilan leading to the martyrdom of Fr. Rhoel Gallardo. Christian civilians have been ambushed and massacred in Lanao del Sur and other places. The MILF has called for a *Jihad*, a holy war. Despite these provocations, our Church leaders have not only tried to discourage Christian vigilante groups from retaliating; above all, they have taken positive steps to promote better relations between Muslims and Christians through prayer services, vigils and through meetings of the Bishops-Ulama Conference. I think this is a laudable path to take because it is in the promotion of better human and community relations that Church people can contribute most towards improving the relations between Christians and our Muslim brothers and sisters in Philippine society. And much more needs to be done before mutual prejudices on both sides can finally be overcome. It is disappointing to hear that so little of Islam is taught in our seminaries even in Mindanao. In fact, this might become a real necessity for all seminarians in the country considering that Muslim communities are sprouting up in different parts of the country including such places as Kalinga in the north.

Before I conclude, allow me, as a Redemptorist, to mention a particular approach that attempts human promotion in the context of mission. I refer to what is known as popular or parish missions as given by Redemptorists in certain parts of the country. In the aftermath of the Philippine revolution against Spanish colonial rule when some 700 friars left the country, hundreds of parishes were left without pastors and some Catholics were defecting to the Aglipayans. The popular missions served at that time the purpose of reaching out to the farthest barrios to bring them the Word of God and the Sacraments, especially the sacraments of baptism, reconciliation and marriage. In many barrios thus missionized, the people were receiving the sacraments after 20 or 30 years of not having seen a priest visit them. And after the mission it could take another 20 to 30 years before they would see another priest in their barrio. I am not exaggerating. Right now our Redemptorist missioners are back in that barrio in Antique where I gave the last mission 30 years ago.

Over the years, the emphasis has changed from delivering the sacraments to the abandoned people in the barrios to evangelization in the context of the formation of basic ecclesial communities (BECs) with a vision of integral or total salvation. This means that we conscienticize the people to become aware of all their needs: socio-economic, cultural, political, religious and pastoral. In the case of San Fernando Parish in Bukidnon, to cite only one example, the mission took up the people's protest against indiscriminate logging and the people's action actually led to the declaration by the national government of a total logging ban in that area.

The problem with this new program is that we now have to spend a much longer time in each place, sometimes a whole year in one parish, drastically cutting down the number of places we can cover. The demand is heavy and we are at a loss how to meet it. One sign of hope is that some religious who had a tradition for this work at the time of the founding of their congregation are now exploring ways of re-engaging themselves once again in mission work. Also, some dioceses where we have given missions have decided to form their own mission team. It is one of our hopes from this National Mission Congress that there be a renewed appreciation for the need to evangelize our own people, even as Filipino missioners go to other lands. Remember what the German review *Herder Korrespondenz* said about the Philippines when we celebrated the fourth centennial of our evangelization in 1965? It described the Philippines as "sacramentalized but not evangelized." Our Redemptorist experience in the far flung barrios would claim that our people are hardly even sacramentalized let alone evangelized! And I have heard Fr. Arévalo express great concern about the critical need for evangelization in our urban areas, for example, in the university belt of Manila.

Finally, I think there are issues that are particularly urgent for our Church in the Philippines when we consider Mission and Human Promotion: **1.** The promotion of the role of women which is developing more rapidly in society than in the Church; **2.** The promotion of the role of lay people, especially the young, both for evangelization and for the social ministry in a Church still predominantly clerical despite our chronic shortage of clergy; **3.** The dissemination of the Church's social doctrine still largely unfamiliar among our educated people, and even among Church people themselves, e.g. the warnings of recent papal encyclicals against exaggerated liberal capitalism in the light of the pervasive advance of economic globalization.

May this National Mission Congress intensify commitment to our mission of evangelization both here and abroad and may that mission lead to authentic human promotion for the realization of God's Kingdom.

MISSION SPIRITUALITY: THE PASCHAL MYSTERY

Daniel Patrick Huang, SJ

I
f "spirituality" refers to the transformed and transforming pattern of life of one who has encountered God in Jesus Christ [1], the focus of our reflection is the *person* of the missioner. After, as it were, having considered the *what* and the *how* of mission in the preceding talks, we now are invited to pay attention to the *who* of mission: the human being who is called to be the agent of mission. What kind of person should he or she be? What style of life, what way of thinking, feeling, and responding should the person who follows Christ in mission have? To use a biblical word, we might ask about the *mind of the missioner:* what kind of "mind" [2], what quality of heart, what general life orientations, should the missioner, particularly the missioner in Asia of the twenty-first century, have?

There will be three parts to our reflection. First, we will reflect on what the mind of the missioner should *not* be. Secondly and more lengthily, we shall meditate on the mind of the missioner as sharing in what St. Paul calls the "mind of Christ." Finally, we shall conclude with a reflection on the paschal mystery.

What the Mind of the Missionary Should Not Be. Following Father Tagle's recommendation the other day, we shall begin with *"illusionectomy"*: an attempt at purging illusions, purifying inadequate mission spiritualities or "mission minds" which, sadly, endure to the present.

What the missionary mind should *not* be became powerfully clear to me the other afternoon when I went to visit, for the first time, the image of the Sto. Niño de Cebu. I was initially moved as I gazed at this image, realizing that this figure of the Christ child was the symbol of the beginning of Christianity in this country. But as I stood before the statue, the ambiguities of the beginnings of Christian mission in the Philippines began to disturb me as well. This beautiful statue of Jesus, powerless in his childhood, had been brought by conquistadors, with the power of arms and violence. Magellan had originally given the statue to the Queen of Cebu in 1521. It was rediscovered in 1565 by Legazpi, during the pillage of Cebu which Legazpi had ordered when Cebu resisted the Spanish military.

Legazpi describes the discovery of the statue in these words: "...One of the soldiers went into a large and well built house of an Indio [sic], where he found an image of the child Jesus (whose most holy name I pray may be universally worshipped). The soldier bowed before it with all reverence and wonder, and brought the image to the place where the other soldiers were. I pray the Holy Name of this image which we have found here, to help us and to grant us victory, in order that these lost people who are ignorant of the precious and rich treasure which was in their possession may come to a knowledge of him" [3]

These are disturbing words when read four centuries after they were written. Despite the undoubted sincerity of Legazpi's piety, his sentiments clearly illustrate the inadequate "missionary mind" memorably described by Japanese theologian Kosuke Koyama as "the teacher complex" and the "crusading mind."

The "teacher complex" refers to a missionary superiority complex that wants to teach, but does not want to learn; that is interested in teaching, but not in being taught; that speaks to people but does not listen to them. It is a mindset of "wealth": I am rich with the truth, which I give you like I give alms to a beggar. It is a "one-way traffic" mind, since all that has meaning and value comes from the teacher [4].

The "crusading mind" is a related mindset. It is a mindset of competition and force that sees Christianity as the sole force of truth and righteousness in a battle against the godlessness, superstition, ignorance and evil "out there." Intent on victory and tangible results usually measured by extension of territory and influence, by numbers, by defeat of rivals, the "crusading mind" assumes a stance of aggressive proselytizing and "bulldozes man and history without appreciation of their complexities" [5].

Sadly, if as Father McCahill shared yesterday, the word "missionary" has come to connote "conquest, violence and disrespect" in Bangladesh as well as in other parts of Asia, it is in large part because of the "teacher complex" and "crusading mind" which informed the activity of many missionaries in Asia in the past. Even more tragically, a little reflection will disclose that these mindsets remain operative and alive among some Christian individuals and groups.

The "Servant Mind" of Jesus Christ. What then should the mind of the missionary be? We must first of all remember that "missionary" is a "participation concept." A missionary or missioner is one who participates in God's dream and project of fullness of life for the world; and thus, the mind of missionary should involve a participation in the mind of the Missioner *par excellence,* Jesus Christ, who did not come with a "teacher complex" nor a "crusading mind"!

Just what exactly is this "mind" of Jesus? In John 13, we read a powerful symbolic description of the inner core of Jesus. Jesus rises from the table and lays aside his garments. Theologians tell us that this "rising and laying aside of garments" is deeply symbolic. Jesus, in doing this, is not simply physically disrobing, but engaged in act of divine revelation. His removal of his outer clothes signals a manifestation of his deepest heart [6]. What is revealed beneath the garments will be the inner heart of Jesus, his "mind." And what is revealed? Underneath the garments are not richly embroidered episcopal vestments, but a towel—the towel of a servant, a towel that gets dirtier and dirtier as Jesus kneels before his friends to wash their feet. What, therefore, is revealed? Saint Paul explains; in Philippians 2, he urges his disciples to "have that *mind* in [them] which was in Christ Jesus: who though he was in the form of God did not regard equality with God something to be grasped at. Rather he emptied himself and took the form of a *servant*." What is revealed is that the Missionary Mind, the mind that participates in the mind of Christ, is a Servant Mind.

Meditating then on Jesus' last symbolic expression of that Servant Mind, the washing of the feet of his disciples on the eve of his death, we discover at least seven qualities of the Servant Mind.

A. During the time of our Lord, a servant washed the feet of a house guest to bid him welcome and to indicate his honored status as guest. Alternately, a disciple too would wash the feet of his Master to show the latter respect. Thus, first of all, Jesus' prophetic action reveals to us that *the servant mind involves* *and is permeated by a spirit of welcome and respect for the people served.* This spirit is a spirit of unconditional welcome and respect, not a spirit of selective respect, which accords different kinds and levels of respect based on human standards of worthiness, importance and dignity, like money and power.

B. Secondly, the act of washing of feet was a hidden, unnoticed act of service. Just as today, one hardly pays attention to a waiter at a restaurant but focuses on one's companions, so the guest, during our Lord's time, would, no doubt, accept the ministrations of the servant, while focusing attention on the *master or host.* Thus, the second quality of the servant mind is that it *is content with hiddenness.* It does not call attention to itself; its service does not need to be noticed or acknowledged. An excessive need for applause and attention on the part of the missioner suggests impurity of motivation, for when attention is focused on the missioner, the attention on the Master is diverted.

C. The German exegete Heinz Schürmann has called attention to the untimely nature of Jesus' footwashing. Normally, during Jesus' time, feet were washed *before* dinner, but Jesus washes feet at an unconventional, unusual time — "while they were at supper." Would it be fanciful to discover in this untimely act of service a third quality of the servant mind? *The servant mind is not ultimately controlled by human calculations and conventions of schedules and agendas; it is flexible enough to allow the times and seasons to be set by the Master.* It is ready to be surprised by the unexpected, the new, the unusual call to service. In short, the servant mind is free: not ultimately clinging to what is simply customary or conventional or familiar; but ready to let go into the "deep waters" of the unknown, the unfamiliar, the untimely, the new.

D. The washing of feet was a service rendered only by the lowest class slaves in Jesus' world. This is not surprising, since the washing of feet was dirty work indeed, involving washing real grime and filth from travel-stained, smelly feet. This fact suggests a fourth quality of the servant mind: *its willingness, indeed its inner compulsion, to go in search of where there is dirt, ugliness, negativity — to wash, to clean and refresh, even if it means being stained by the dirt in the process.* A servant who is too "clean," who is untouched or unaffected by the dirt and ugliness that mar people's lives — their pain, their anguish, their confusion, their sin — has not yet assimilated the servant mind of Jesus.

E. When we read John 13, Jesus' dialogue with Peter shows how poorly, once again, this greathearted, but flawed disciple has understood his Master's intentions and meanings. Further, Jesus alludes to the fact that "not all are clean," implying by these words his betrayer Judas. The fact that Jesus washes the feet of one who misunderstands him and of another who betrays him indicates a fifth quality of the servant mind. *The servant mind continues in graciousness and self-giving even in the face of misunderstanding and rejection.* It continues to give even when there is no appreciation. It is ready to "love in the darkness," as it were. It surrenders to the Holy Mystery of God its need for assurance of effectivity or success; and continues to be faithful even in apparent failure.

F.   After he has washed his disciples' feet, Jesus goes on to exhort them to wash each other's feet, in imitation of him. Here we find a sixth quality of the servant mind: *the servant mind awakens servanthood in the ones served.* A missioner does not desire to keep his or her people in a state of perpetual dependence; rather, like Jesus, it is the servant's goal to awaken, to inspire a similar spirit of self-donation in those served.

G.   Finally, one's attention is drawn by the detailed description of Jesus' act of service at this last meal with his friends. The Gospels are generally reserved, even at times frustratingly silent with regard to details. We do not know how Jesus looked; we have no descriptions of his voice, his stature, his appearance. By way of contrast, here we are supplied with a multitude of tiny details that allow us to see with clarity in our mind's eye what Jesus does: how he rises from table, how he removes his outer garments, how he wraps a towel around his waist, how he washes his friends' feet and wipes them dry with a towel. Why this surprising detail? Perhaps, this suggests that *servanthood claims all the little details of one's life.* Servanthood need not seek heroic circumstances for its expression, but can and must be lived in the little, seemingly insignificant details that make up one's life.

The Paschal Mind of the Missioner.   Our reflection has thus far clarified that, for our time and our world of Asia, the missionary mind must be purified of attitudes described as the "teacher complex" and "the crusading mind." Secondly, we have contemplated the mind of Jesus revealed by his radiant act of service before his death, the washing of his disciples' feet. We have discerned seven qualities of his servant mind, seven characteristics too of "missionary spirituality," of missionary life-orientation and practice.

We close our reflection with a word on the "paschal mystery" which is the ultimate context of meaningfulness of all we have said about the servant mind of Jesus and his follower in mission. What is the "paschal mystery"? Theological "code" for the saving event of Jesus' death and resurrection, the "paschal mystery" reveals two important truths. First, the paschal mystery reveals that God's deepest desire is to fill the world with his overflowing, abundant life. Secondly, the paschal mystery discloses the *manner* by which God fills the world with life: namely, through death. The Good News of Jesus' death and resurrection is not so much life *after* death, but life *through* death. Life, the life God desires to fill this hungry world with, is given, when, as with Jesus, life is poured out. Even the quickest reflection on our own lives should convince us of these twin truths of the Paschal Mystery. All that is alive and good in us is the result of someone dying for us—someone dying to self, sacrificing and forgetting self, so that life may spring up in us. Conversely, I think we will see that all that is dead and deadening in us is the result of a refusal to die, on the part of others, and also, on the part of ourselves.

What is the point of all this? The seven points of the servant mind described above all involve self-forgetfulness, self-emptying, self-gift, dying—to comfort, to security, to privilege—for the sake of life. The servant mind then is a paschal mind; the spirituality of the missioner is the spirituality of the paschal mystery. To seek, for our time and world, to live the servant mind and heart of Jesus, is ultimately to live a life of life-giving dying. Missionary spirituality as the living out of the servant mind, thus involves the great gift of playing a part with Jesus, by the power of his life-transforming Spirit, in the Father's project of bringing the fullness of life to this world.

---

[1] For this articulation of what spirituality is, cf. Mark A. McKintosh, *Mystical Theology: The Integrity of Spirituality and Theology* (Oxford: Blackwell, 1998), 9: "I propose thinking of spirituality as the new and transformative pattern of life and thought engendered in people by their encounter with God."

[2] Cf. Brendan Bryne's commentary on Philippians 2:5: "Have this *mind* among you which was in Christ Jesus": "The Gk *phronein* in Paul's usage goes beyond rational reflection to include the 'mindset' that issues in a determined pattern of behavior." Brendan Byrne, "Philippians," in *The New Jerome Biblical Commentary*, ed. Raymond Brown, Joseph Fitzmyer, Roland Murphy (London: Chapman, 1993): 794.

[3] From John Schumacher, S.J., *Readings in Philippine Church History.*

[4] Kosuke Koyama, *Three Mile an Hour God* (Maryknoll: Orbis), 51-55.

[5] Kosuke Koyama, *Waterbuffalo Theology* (Maryknoll: Orbis), 223-24.

[6] Cf. John Shea, *Gospel Light* (New York: Crossroad, 1988), 147.

Part Five

HOMILIES

AND

REFLECTIONS

Eucharistic Homilies

HOMILY: RICARDO J. CARDINAL VIDAL:

With the gospel we have just read, we are immediately given the right direction to take as we begin the National Mission Congress this evening. It reminds us that, first and foremost, we are here because we all wish to be followers of our Lord Jesus Christ. Are we? That is why we have come from far and near; that is why we gather here in this city of Señor Santo Niño....

This is a "mission" congress that we are privileged to attend, actively and effectively. And at once, let us not forget that it is "his mission" that is "our mission." True? We are not the source of the mission, we are only sent. For Jesus himself has said this, "As the Father has sent me, so I am sending you."

Mission therefore is not just "words that we preach"; it is more so, "life that gives witness to Christ." When we look at mission this way, then we realize how blessed Pedro Calungsod, a noble son of the Church of Cebu, convincingly proclaimed the good news of Christ to the people of the Marianas Islands.

"Beato Pedro," as we fondly call him here in Cebu, did not only proclaim the gospel with words. He courageously gave witness to Christ even to the point of dying for his faith. And for this, he becomes for us a model and an example of a true missionary. You and I may not be called like Beato Pedro to die for our faith;

but certainly, each and everyone of us, as "baptized persons" is called to "live up" to its demands as mentioned by the gospel today: that of denying oneself, taking up our cross daily, and following the steps of Christ.

As we begin this National Mission Congress and prompted by the challenge of the gospel reading, let us make a clear response, as people of God in the Philippines, to what our bishops have called us: "that we may be truly missionary in spirit and action." Let us renew all our efforts to "tell the world of His love."

HOMILY: APOSTOLIC NUNCIO ANTONIO FRANCO:

Maayong hapon kaninyong tanan! I consider it both an honor and privilege to be with you here at the National Mission Congress. I greet you with all much affection, hope and with great joy. None of us can be in any doubt as to how meaningful this moment is, and what incalculable potential it contains. Your bishops have chosen to make of this Congress—the first of its kind in your history as Church—the principal celebration of the Great Jubilee of the Year 2000. Thus, we may say that there are focused here in Cebu—like many rays of the sun—all the prayers, initiatives, pilgrimages, graces, and blessings that have been and are part of your jubilee journey. We hope that this Congress will see the Church in the Philippines truly set aflame with the fire of the Spirit, who is always the initiator and actor of mission.

Today, too, we are blessed to be celebrating the feast of San Lorenzo Ruiz, martyr, whose courageous witness to the faith is for us a rich source of inspiration. Lovingly and proudly, we keep his memory in the biblical sense of rejoicing in his being fully alive in the Lord, rejoicing in his communion with us and his on-going concern and involvement in the mission entrusted to every single Filipino Catholic. San Lorenzo Ruiz is here with us in Cebu, urging us to live our mission now with the same courage that once was his....

This National Mission Congress is an especially providential moment for the Church in the Philippines to appropriate ever more completely the Holy Father's message in his Apostolic Exhortation, *Ecclesia in Asia*. There Pope John Paul II speaks repeatedly of Jesus as gift, the gift to be shared. For example, he says: "the great question now facing the Church in Asia"—and we can read "in the Philippines"—"is how to share with our Asian brothers and sisters what we treasure as the gift containing all gifts, namely, the Good News of Jesus Christ"

(19). And again, "to bear witness to Jesus Christ is the supreme service which the Church can offer to the peoples of Asia, for it responds to their profound longing for the Absolute, and it unveils the truths and values which will ensure their integral human development" (20)....

The Church all over and also in the Philippines is facing a widespread spiritual and cultural uncertainty, as evidenced by the ambivalence of moral and spiritual stance of Filipino Catholics on issues affecting their daily lives and by the dichotomy that often exists between the life of faith and social, political and economic life. You have initiated a response to this challenge, ten years ago, through the Second Plenary Council of the Philippines in which you have resolved to retell the story of Jesus in our time and undertake a program of renewed integral evangelization....

Needless to say however, that the Congress will also issue a call for a redoubled commitment of the Church in the Philippines to worldwide and *ad gentes* mission, in its *ad extra* dimension. "The Church's faith in Jesus is a gift received and a gift to be shared; it is the greatest gift which the Church can offer to Asia" (EA 10). Your history, culture and experience have made you a people of travelers. Now, more than ever, when you travel, travel in the Lord's name, to make him known and loved to the ends of the earth. Your Church is already making a significant contribution in terms of personnel and resources to worldwide mission, but Jesus, the Missionary, is offering you the grace of being more generous in your response to his call to walk with him in the proclamation of the Good News. The peoples of Asia need Jesus Christ and his Gospel. The Church in her one ambition is to continue his mission of service and love, so that all Asians may have life and have it abundantly....

HOMILY: CBCP PRESIDENT ORLANDO B. QUEVEDO:

If I asked you who are the evangelists, what answer would you give? I suppose you would say: Mark, Matthew, Luke and John. But, technically, an evangelist is one who announces the Good News, the Gospel. So all of us who announce the Gospel are on a mission of evangelizing. We are all evangelists.

Let us not forget the angels, whose feast we celebrate today. For instance, the angel Gabriel appeared to the Virgin Mary and announced the Good News of Jesus, the Son of God, the Savior of the world. Gabriel announced that Jesus is mission, that Jesus is being sent from the Father to be born of the Virgin Mary....

We even see that there was an involvement of angels in the mission of Jesus.... The devil, a fallen angel, tried to dissuade Jesus from doing his mission in the way that his Father told him to do it: in the way of powerlessness, humility, simplicity, in the way of servanthood. The Father wanted his Son to demonstrate to the world his Sonship, not in the way we understand it, but in the way that God alone understands, in the way of humility, of suffering obedience, of poverty and powerlessness....

In the beginning of his mission, Jesus was tempted by the devil three times. The devil failed, but he tempted him again before his crucifixion—through the prince of the apostles. Peter remonstrated with Jesus: "Lord, you shall not go to Jerusalem, you shall not die, you shall not be killed, you shall not be crucified on the cross." And what did Jesus tell Peter? "Get behind me, Satan." The temptation in the desert was repeated through Peter. Jesus accomplishes his mission through his crucifixion and death....

What is the message of the angels to those who are involved in actualizing the mission of Jesus? Generally, the message of the angels in the New Testament is: "Be not afraid." Be not afraid, Zechariah, because your prayer has been heard. Be not afraid, Joseph, to take Mary as your wife. Be not afraid, shepherds of Bethlehem, for I bring you good news of great joy. Be not afraid, Mary of Magdalene, Jesus has risen from the dead. And, it is the same message to us: Be not afraid! ... And on this feast of Saints Gabriel, Rafael, and Michael, I repeat these same words to you, my brothers and sisters: "Be not afraid. Declare and proclaim the loving work of God in Jesus. Go, tell the world of His Love."

HOMILY: ARCHBISHOP JAIME L. CARDINAL SIN:

My homily today will be by my own choice very, very simple, but I do want to leave a word with you which I believe lays a charge on you, which asks for a commitment from you. It is fitting that this "new Pentecost for Mission"—our National Mission Congress—shall place its last full day, this Saturday, under the holy patronage of Mary, "Queen of the Missions and Mother of all missionaries." We are all sure, I believe, that she is with us in a special way today. And we want to tell her today, how much we want her to be with us.

The Upper Room and Pentecost, we have always taught, are: the birthplace and the birthday of the Church. It is also, we may say, the birth of the mission *ad gentes*.... We want to remember that Mary was there, in the Upper Room in the midst of the Apostles, and from the Fathers of the Church to our own time we have hailed Mary as Mother of the Church, the Mother of all Christians. Today we want to remind ourselves that when the Spirit came down upon this "early Church," Mary was at its center....

Rightly, then, have the Latin American bishops given Our Lady the title, "Morning Star of Evangelization"—a title which the Second Plenary Council of the Philippines (PCP-II) also made its own.... What is not as much known, however, is the crucial role our blessed Mother played in the Christianization [of the Philippines] which was "an achievement without parallel in history." It has been established, we believe, that Our blessed Lady in some ways "went ahead" of her Son in winning our ancestors to the Gospel and the Church. ...historians tell us that from the start the "early Filipinos" rallied so spontaneously around Mary the Mother, loved the rosary and other Marian devotions, took her to their hearts with such a remarkable welcoming affection....

And now you ask me, what does all this have to do with mission, what does all this have to do with this stirring congress where we hear the Holy Father saying, "I wish to tell you of my special desire: that the Filipinos will become the foremost missionaries of the Church in Asia"? ...Our special gift in mission will be our love of Our blessed Lady. ...Today we rededicate our heart to her, as we assume "the missionary mandate and task" in the Asia of the Third Millennium.

HOMILY: PAPAL LEGATE JOHN BAPTIST CARDINAL WU:

This Mission Congress has helped to clarify our *vision* of what *mission* means. It has shown us how *to think globally, act locally and live contemplatively*.... It is often said that contemplatives are the *spiritual power house* of the Church. So, it is fitting that we close this Mission Congress on the Feast of Saint Therese of the Child Jesus, a contemplative who never left her convent, and yet was proclaimed *Patroness of the Missions*. Through her prayers and sacrifices and with the *power of the Spirit*, she accompanies the many Missionaries who "go forth" on missionary journeys and undertake mission labors proclaiming the Good News of Jesus Christ. Here we can say that contemplatives show us how to *think globally, act locally and live contemplatively*, for *they* are the *power* of the missionary effort of the Church. In the Holy Father's words, "the future of mission depends to a great extent on contemplation. Unless the missionary is a contemplative he cannot proclaim Christ in a credible way. He is a witness to the experience of God" (*Redemptoris Missio* 91).

Last Thursday, we celebrated the Feast day of the first Filipino Saint—Saint Lorenzo Ruiz. I well remember that, at the Beatification Ceremony in 1981, the *theme* in small print on the back of the missalette, struck me forcefully then and still does now. It was: "*to die for the faith is a gift to some, to live the faith is a call to all.*" What a *theme*! How inspiring and challenging, frightening and heartening!...

The Holy Father emphasized that: "missionary activity renews the Church, revitalizes faith and Christian identity, and offers fresh enthusiasm and new incentive. *Faith is strengthened when it is given to others!*" (*Redemptoris Missio*, 2). After his Resurrection, Jesus said to the apostles: "As the Father has sent me, even so I send you" (John 20:21). Before his Ascension, Jesus told the apostles, "Go into all the world and preach the Gospel to the whole creation" (Mark 16:15) "and make disciples of all nations" (Matthew 28:19). Having received the Holy Spirit on the day of Pentecost, the apostles proclaimed the Gospel and spread the Kingdom of God to the ends of the earth (cf. Acts 1:8)....

Dear brothers and sisters, to quote Bishop Ramon C. Arguelles, "*Filipinos everywhere! Learn you Faith, Live your Faith, Share your Faith.*" What a Vision and Mission! What a Right and Duty! What an honor and privilege!

REFLECTION ON WITNESS OF LIFE

FORMER PRESIDENT CORAZON C. AQUINO:

Allow me to share with you today some of Ninoy's experiences in prison, which I believe contributed to his spiritual transformation.... Let me quote a few lines from Ninoy's letter to Soc Rodrigo:

"I prayed the rosary. The mysteries started me on my meditation. It was the life of Christ from birth to the ascension. Suddenly, Jesus became a living human being. His life was to become my inspiration. Here was a God-Man who preached nothing but love and was rewarded with death. Here was a God-Man who had power over all creation but took the mockery of a crown of thorns with humility and patience. And for all His noble intentions, he was shamed, vilified, slandered and betrayed.

"Then it dawned on me how puny were my sufferings compared to Him whose only purpose was to save mankind from eternal damnation. Then, as if I heard a voice tell me: Why do you cry? I have gifted you with consolations, honors and glory which have been denied to the millions of your countrymen. I made you the youngest war correspondent, presidential assistant, Mayor, Vice-Governor, Governor and Senator of the Republic, and I recall you never thanked me for all these gifts. I have given you a full life, a great wife and beautiful lovable children. Now that I visit you with a slight desolation, you cry and whimper like a spoiled brat!

"With this realization, I went down on my knees begged His forgiveness. I know that I was merely undergoing a test, maybe in preparation for another mission. I know everything that happens in this world is with His knowledge and consent. I knew He would not burden me with a load I could not carry. I therefore resigned my self to His will."

...I cannot, of course, tell you how all these changes took place inside Ninoy. I saw only their effects—particularly the spiritual repose he had attained and that was manifested in his words and actions.... Ninoy came home as a man of peace with a message of peace and reconciliation. That he was met with violence makes him no less a man of peace and his message no less a message of peace.... Ninoy was prevented from pursuing his personal quest for a peaceful solution to our nation's ills. But he did succeed in awakening a great number of our countrymen out of their apathy, indifference and fear....

We cannot attain peaceful resolution of conflict by ourselves alone—there is need to pray to Him who is the source of peace, love and all that is good. But we must be humbly patient in prayer.... In times of trial and tribulation, I hope that we will learn to accept suffering as a part of our life in and with Christ. As Saint Paul said in his letter to the Corinthians: "I am content with weaknesses, insults, hardships, persecutions, and difficulties for Christ's sake. For when I am weak, then I am strong" (cf. II Corinthians 12:10). Thank you and good morning!

Part Six

OFFICIAL

DOCUMENTS

Message of the First National Mission Congress

INTRODUCTION

TO OUR BELOVED BROTHERS AND SISTERS:

We, the participants of the First National Mission Congress, have gathered at Cebu City, from 27 September to 01 October in this Jubilee Year 2000 of the Lord's Incarnation, in response to its convocation by the Catholic Bishops' Conference of the Philippines. The beginning of the Third Christian Millennium, which our Holy Father named "the Asian Millennium," has reminded us that nearly four billion Asians have not yet truly encountered the "living Jesus—our crucified and risen Lord" and that it is our joy and duty as Christians to proclaim His Name and His Gospel to all times, to all places, to all human situations and spaces which have not yet heard his Word of Salvation, to all human persons to whom His love has not been told. This is the challenge the Church has placed before us in fulfillment of a divine calling discerned in faith within our history as a people.

PART ONE

In the 16th century, explorers and missionaries from Spain brought us the Gospel and the Church. Our ancestors took so readily to the Christian faith that in the first evangelization of our people, what was accomplished in some forty years—the Christianization of almost all our ancestral communities—has been called an achievement without equal in all of the Church's mission history. Surely we may see in this the plan of God's providence, a vocation of our people to faith, a vocation to become the people of the Father of our Lord Jesus Christ, "God's own people" in this part of the earth.

This was, and is, a vocation also and necessarily to become a "Church-in-mission" for Asian peoples around us, and beyond; a vocation whose hour of grace, whose *kairos* now sounds for Filipino Christians, the hour of the Lord's call and command, spoken directly to us: "Go, therefore, and make disciples of all peoples...."

In this Congress, we have opened ourselves to this call, spoken to us by the Spirit of Jesus and by His holy Church. We accepted it, for all of "God's people" in our country, whom we, representatives of every diocese, prelature, vicariate and church-circumscription in the Catholic Church in this country, represent in this Congress.

In this Congress, we have thanked God for this most precious gift: the gift to receive Jesus and to experience Him; the gift to belong to Jesus, to bear Jesus in our persons, to bring Jesus to all the world—this world that God loves so greatly and so unconditionally.

In this Congress, we have cherished and celebrated this gift; we have rejoiced in this gift because it is a call to live His life with Him, to love people as He has loved them, to serve them—especially "the little ones" with whom He has identified Himself—to spend our lives for them, so that they too "may have life and have it more abundantly."

In this Congress, we have tried to hear, with all our minds and hearts, the words with which Jesus calls us:

"For God so loved the world that He sent His only Son, not to condemn the world, but that the world might be saved by Him."

"The Spirit of the Lord is upon me, because he has anointed me to bring good news to the poor; He has sent me to proclaim release to captives, and recovery of sight to the blind, to let the oppressed go free, and to proclaim the year of the Lord's favor."

"May they be one in us, so that the world may believe that you have sent me; ...may they become perfectly one, so that the world may know that you have sent me."

"Go, therefore, and make disciples of all nations, baptizing them in the name of the Father, and of the Son, and of the Holy Spirit, teaching them to observe all that I have commanded you."

We have tried to make these words resound within us, in prayer and desire, so that we may be obedient to them in love, so that we may say, HERE WE ARE, LORD JESUS, send us in your Name.

PART TWO

And thus, in this Congress, we wish to "receive and make ours" formally and explicitly, the Pastoral Letter of our Bishops, on the Church's Mission in the New Millennium (5 July 2000). It is their own valuable meditation on our people's providential vocation to Christian Mission, and their recognition of the present hour when this vocation comes to its time of full realization and fulfillment. Every part of this Pastoral Letter has much to teach us, and we will read it and reflect on it more and more in days to come.

With our Bishops we wish to affirm:

— that we believe that each of us, by baptism and confirmation, become true sharers of the mission of Jesus; every Christian is a missionary by worship and work, by word and witness, by our whole lives;

— that we believe that every Christian community—family, neighborhood, every parish and diocese; every covenant community, every BEC, even every Christian gathering, is and must be missionary, because it is part of the missionary Body of Christ on earth;

— that we believe that in fulfilling this vocation, we must "keep our eyes on Jesus," walk His way of mission even as He walked it, in unfeigned service and lowliness of heart, in poverty, in powerlessness, in the path of His passion, death and resurrection, for all true mission is authentic sharing in His paschal mystery, in total loving and self gift;

— that we believe that this vocation-to-mission must be realized "AT HOME"—in our own country, wherever we live and play, work and suffer, in all of Philippine society, which at this time must be deeply, broadly and really re-evangelized, because the profound and rapid changes in our nation—affecting especially our young people—confront us with vast challenges to our Christian faith and our Christian life today;

— that we believe that we as Filipino Catholics are also sent as missionaries *AD GENTES*, to peoples around us, in the great continent of Asia and beyond, peoples who have not yet received the great gift of Jesus and the incredible Good News of His Gospel. We believe further that the hour of this sending is NOW, and we beg the Holy Spirit to come to us "as mighty wind and tongues of flame" so that we may go forth in His name and by His power with the courage and hope that are also His gifts.

CONCLUSION

We thank the Most Holy Triune God, Father, Son, and Spirit, for all that this Mission Congress has given us. And as we end we turn to our Mother Mary, Mother of the Lord, Mother of our people, Queen of the Apostles. She was the Morning Star of Evangelization in our country, in a way almost unique and un-paralleled in Christian history. She, more than any other, led our ancestors to faith in her Son. It is she who, over the centuries, has more than anyone else kept our people despite trial and turmoil and turbulence, faithful to her Son. Now we ask her to stand beside us in this moment of decision and deed. We ask her, Mother of Asian peoples, to lead us all, surely and safety to the Way, the Truth and the Life. He who is her Son, whose love embraced the world from the cross, and who now at the right hand of the Father, intercedes for us, until we, all humankind—find ourselves, one at last, in the kingdom of God, to whom be glory and honor through all the ages.

And so we pray:

Lord Jesus Christ, You are our Way, our Truth, and our Life. Strengthen our faith in your word, our hope in your promises, and love for you and one another. Make us living witnesses of faith to our own people, and give us the gift and the courage to proclaim your Name to those who do not know you, to dialogue with people of other faiths, and to build an earthly city of peace, justice and love.

Holy Spirit, Lord and Giver of Life, on the day of Pentecost, you came to the disciples of Christ and accompany them with your power as they went about to preach the Gospel and baptize those who believe. Teach us to value the Christian doctrine and way of life, to be attentive to your word, and to be eager for your sacraments, so that as we set forth to proclaim our faith in Jesus Christ we may be worthy vessels of divine life. Amen.

+ARCHBISHOP ORLANDO B. QUEVEDO, OMI
Archbishop of Cotabato
President, CBCP
October 1, 2000

"MISSIONS" AND THE CHURCH IN THE PHILIPPINES

A PASTORAL LETTER ON THE CHURCH'S MISSION IN THE NEW MILLENNIUM

INTRODUCTION

*G*o to the people of all nations and make them my disciples, baptizing them in the name of the Father, and of the Son and of the Holy Spirit and teach them to do everything I have taught you. I will be with you always even unto the end of the world* (Matthew 28:19-20).

Recalling this great commission of Jesus, the Second Plenary Council of the Philippines in February 1991 affirmed that the Lord's words have a special resonance for us, the Church in the Philippines, since the Philippines is the country in Asia with the largest Catholic population. PCP-II speaks of the Philippine Church as "a communion in a state of mission" because "the community of disciples does not exist only for itself.... It exists for the world" (103-104).

PCP-II also reminded us that Pope John Paul II spoke with a special clarity when he said to the Philippine bishops in 1981, "There is no doubt about it: the Philippines has a special missionary vocation to proclaim the Good News, to carry the light of Christ to the nations." And in January 1995, Pope John Paul II at World Youth Day called Catholics in the Philippines and Asia to proclaim Christ, his Gospel, his love to Asia. His renewed summons for the Church in the Philippines was in direct continuity with the often reiterated declaration of *a special vocation to mission*, specially in Asia, given by the Roman Pontiffs, (at least) from Pope Pius XI to our time: all the Popes of our time have spoken of this Philippine vocation-to-mission.

Then, in November 1999 at New Delhi, the Holy Father, promulgating his Apostolic Exhortation *Ecclesia in Asia*, declared that the new millennium is the new millennium for Asia, when we must proclaim Christ, his Gospel, his love, to billions of Asians who have not yet come to know Jesus.

With the foregoing as context, we, the Bishops of the Philippines, address this pastoral letter to Catholics in our country, as the new millennium of Christianity opens. Our letter looks forward to the *National Mission Congress in Cebu* this September 27 to October 1, which we hope and pray will be one of the most significant events of this Holy Year of Jubilee in our country.

PART ONE: **THE MISSION SCENARIO**

The Holy Father and the Asian Bishops tell us that this moment of history presents us with this amazing reality: about two-thirds of humanity today, i.e. some four billion people, make up the vast portion of the world which the Special Synod of Asia in 1998 included. Here live four billions of people, in an "intricate mosaic of many cultures, languages, beliefs and traditions." Christians make up only about three percent of this truly immense mass of humankind, only some 125 millions. We could say that, roughly speaking, 97% of Asia has not yet come "to the knowledge of Christ and His Gospel of God's love and grace." Thus the task of the Church in Asia, as she crosses the threshold of the new millennium, is to proclaim God's Word to Asian peoples, "*to tell the world of His love.*" That is, to make known to our brothers and sisters in Asia, to share with them as gifts we have received, the person of Jesus, the grace of His Spirit, His good news of unbounded compassion and love for sinful humanity, of communion in God's own life, in truth and freedom, in solidarity and peace.

Of the 125 million Christians in Asia, some 70 millions are Filipinos, that is, more than one-half are from our country. It is clear that the challenge of proclaiming Christ in Asia is a summons addressed *first of all* to us, to share the gift of faith that we ourselves received. It is a challenge we cannot refuse: surely at this moment of history the Lord is calling us. "The harvest is great, the laborers are few. Come with me to the golden fields of harvest." The hour of that challenge is now. Now is the *kairos*, the hour of the Lord's call. And "the grace of the hour" is now.

We believe that, surely, there was a divine providence at work in our turbulent history, leading our people through centuries of struggle and suffering to the present hour. Through this, Filipinos kept their faith alive, enduring and even joyful, devoted to the Jesus of Bethlehem, Calvary and Easter morning, "in love with our Mother Mary" (*pueblo amante de Maria*). With deep gratitude we wish to cite the labors of the foreign missionaries who were God's instruments in planting the seed of the Faith among our people. So that now, as the 21st century begins, despite all the forces that have tried to destroy the Faith we have received and made our own, we can yet clearly hear the summons which the Lord of history and the Church address to us, showing us the immensity of Asian multitudes, and bidding us to "*tell the world of His love.*"

PART TWO: **EVERY CHRISTIAN IS A MISSIONARY**

Every Christian is called to take part in the mission of Jesus, and the mission the Church has received from him. Baptism inserts us into Christ and to the body of Christ, which is the Church. Baptism inserts us into the Christ-life, calls us to his discipleship, calls to take part in Christian mission to the world in our time. Every baptized Christian is thus called to believe in the Gospel of Jesus, to make it his/her own, to respond to it and to live it out integrally in his/her life.

This call is also a call to the community, which the Spirit of Jesus indwells, the community which, in each one's own place and time, is Christ's Body, the Church. In this community one learns to commit himself/herself to the work of Christ and His Church in the world; one is called to respond to his/her own vocation within God's plan of salvation. Each is called into the mission of Jesus, and under the Spirit, one is invited to take part in God's redeeming work in history. Thus Vatican II (*Ad Gentes*, 2) teaches that mission is intrinsic to Christianity, and that to be Christian is to be missionary.

Every Christian is thus asked to follow Jesus-in-mission. Jesus himself described His own mission in the terms we find in the Gospel of Luke (Luke 4:18-19): "*The Spirit of the Lord is upon me, because he has anointed me to bring good news to the poor. He has sent me to proclaim release to captives, and the recovery of sight to the blind, to let the oppressed go free, and to proclaim the year of the Lord's favor."*

Here Jesus gives us his own personal job-description, so to speak; this is his own mission statement. This text is also a basic mission statement for every Christian, because our mission is to follow in the footsteps of Jesus-in-mission.

The "great commission" of Matthew 28:19-20, the solemn sending forth of the Eleven, is addressed first of all to the leadership of the Church. However, Christians of all times have seen in this classic Gospel text a missionary mandate addressed to the whole Church. It tells the disciples to "go," to move from where they are, to "the nations, the peoples." It tells them to "teach, baptize, make disciples." And as Jesus says "go," he promises, "I am with you always, until the end of time."

Here then are two great mission texts found in the Gospel. The message and meaning of both Matthew 28 and Luke 4 must be heard by all of us, for they describe what mission means for all. Both texts challenge us to continue the mission which Jesus received from his Father and which he hands on to us, for our own time and place, in this moment of human history.

Mission, then, cannot but be "outgoing." It is a "reaching-out ministry": in Jesus' own life, his ministry was his exercise of mission. He went first to his own people to proclaim the message of the Kingdom to them, reaching out to all of them, especially to "the lost sheep of Israel." He went to the nearby towns and places, "so that I can proclaim the message there also, for this is what I came out to do" (Mark 1:38). But "outgoing and reaching out" do not have a primarily geographical meaning, as if there is mission only if it takes place in "faraway places with strange-sounding names." Missionary activity can (at least in a wider sense) take place wherever one is situated, as long as there is a reaching out to others for the sake of God's Kingdom.

We want to insist that every Christian is a missionary by his/her baptism and confirmation. What we do, at home or in "other places" at the service of the Kingdom of God can be called both ministry and mission, mission at least in its most fundamental sense. In such mission, we actualize the truth that we are bearers of Christ and his Gospel wherever we may live and work, and that we are keepers of our brothers and sisters in the love of Christ.

Such mission is possible for all, for lay Christians especially, whatever their state of life and personal situation might be, even if they cannot engage "full time" in it, even if they have not received ordination in the Church, even if they do not live the life of the vows of religious. The Spirit calls all the baptized to participate in the ministry and mission of Jesus. The Spirit inspires all who will open their hearts, calls them to let Christ enter into their daily lives and activities. The Spirit sets them free to join in renewing and transforming the milieu in which they live and work, and the greater world of humankind around us—to the measure of their gifts, their capabilities and possibilities, according to the grace given to each one. As sons and daughters of the Church we are bidden to exercise and to share the Faith, Hope and Love that are God's gift to us, through the Christ-life he has given to us.

PART THREE: THE CHURCH IN THE PHILIPPINES – CALLED TO MISSION

The Federation of Asian Bishops' Conferences (FABC) has for more than 25 years tried to articulate again and again what response the Church in Asia should give to the Lord's call to mission. It is the purpose of the National Mission Congress this year that we, the Church in the Philippines, may gather together at Cebu and undertake a life-task for this *kairos*, this hour of grace given us as the People of God journeying with our Asian brothers and sisters toward his kingdom.

We as Church are called to be in our part of the globe "the universal sacrament of salvation," sent out by the Lord on a mission to the whole of the human race (*Lumen Gentium* 13). The Church universal is Catholic because of this mission. Hence to each local Church the mandate is also given to proclaim Jesus' message and invitation, to give living witness of God's love in Christ Jesus, and to share the gifts it has received from the Lord. For the Church in the Philippines, for every one of our local Churches, there is a new insistence and a new urgency to fulfill this mandate.

We believe that in recent years the Spirit has awakened among us a new awareness of the Church's missionary task, and has also poured out his gifts to begin to realize it in deed and in truth. For in recent decades, a constantly increasing number of our brothers and sisters—priests, religious brothers and sisters, lay people—have left our shores to share their Faith with peoples of other lands, in every continent on the face of the earth. The Mission Society of Philippines has sent several priests as missionaries in many parts of the world.

Many Filipino priests, brothers and sisters, belonging to different religious congregations as well as diocesan priests are now working in the foreign missions.
Several lay missionaries, both men and women, who underwent training through
the Catholic Lay Mission Program, are also working in the foreign missions. New
movements of faith such as the covenant communities, initiated by the Filipino
laity under the inspiration of the Holy Spirit, have spread to particular churches
of other countries and have surely contributed to the efforts of evangelization
of those sister churches. Our overseas workers have in so many instances become missionaries, bringing the Gospel and faith where these have not been
present, renewing and reactivating Christian life and practice where these have
been in decline. Through Radio Veritas Asia, based in Manila, the saving message
of Christ has reached millions of people living in many parts of the vast continent. May we not see in these events the hand of the Lord, and the movement
of his Providence?

It is imperative then that we—all of us—renew our own understanding of
mission. We urge most especially the formators of our seminarians, the candidates for the priesthood, to help the future leaders of the Church to develop a
personal and profound understanding of mission during their priestly formation. Our young priests should experience life in the missions either here or
abroad so that they can become effective agents of renewal in mission consciousness among the faithful.

Mission is the proclamation of the Good news of salvation given by the
Father in Christ Jesus. It is about the forgiveness, the communion, peace and
hope Christ brought to us for all time, and unto everlasting life. Mission is the
sharing of the promise of a new heaven and a new earth, the ultimate triumph
of life over death, of grace and glory over evil and sin in the new Jerusalem
which will be given to us by God. But mission does not proclaim only God's
victory in the life to come, but also the redemption of time and history in the
cross and resurrection of Jesus. Mission is about the presence and action of the
power of the Spirit of Jesus in the struggles against sinfulness in the heart of
humanity, in individual lives and in the relationships and structures of injustice,
domination and alienation which sin establishes in society. In our present context mission will therefore mean the elimination of graft and corruption and the
active pursuit of peace. For mission is about creating and transforming communities that shall live in God's *shalom*, communities of truth and justice, of solidarity, freedom and love.

PART FOUR: SOME REFLECTIONS ON OUR CALL TO MISSION

1. *The Mission of Jesus:* Since Christian mission is a "following in the footsteps of Jesus," we need to return to the person and ministry of Jesus as the Gospels reveal him to us. If we lose sight of Jesus we may lose our way. Perhaps we may simply remember that Jesus' mission was rooted in his "incredible intimacy" with *Abba,* his Father. All mission begins in that experience of *Abba,* in that unique relationship with the Father in heaven. It is there, then, in our own relationship with the Father, that our mission is rooted; we may never forget this. This is one reason why *prayer is itself the fountainhead of mission.*

Jesus, "the one sent by the Father," (cf. John 4:34; 20:21) is the first missionary. His mission is, under the Spirit's guidance, constantly concerned with the concrete needs of people's real lives (cf. Luke 4:16-19). Then, we are not to forget that Jesus' major attention was focused on the formation of his disciples. As we read the Gospels we realize that in a true sense this seemed to be his over-riding, even his primary concern. It tells us that we are also called to give primacy to formation for mission, not only for those who will "go abroad," but for all of us who will "stay at home." We must form *true missionary attitudes* within our families and communities, precisely because for most of us, our very living-out of Christian life, our witness, will be our real missionary labor! Being constantly guided by the Spirit must be a radical attitude in our lives. In choosing priorities for our action, we see that Jesus gave so much of his attention to healing the sick, to comforting the afflicted and the sorrowing, to showing mercy to sinners, to turning to children and youth, to a "preferential love for the poor and the little ones" in society, the marginalized and "left out," for those who were powerless and needing compassion. Mission history's most inspiring pages teach us of Christian missionaries acting as Jesus did, and in our time we have the unforgettable figure of Mother Teresa of Calcutta to tell us that this manner of mission inspires and moves even the most secularized sectors of modern society.

2. *Mission in Asia.* There is a sense in which mission in Asia today will reproduce in a new way the missionary mind and heart of Jesus—that "mind which was in Christ Jesus" (Philippians 2:6 ff.): the self-abnegation of his entire life, his acceptance—even his choice—of a life of seeming insignificance and powerlessness in the eyes of the world; his acceptance of failure, of the final rejection of his work, offered in self-sacrificing love. Jesus' mission was met with persecution, it ended in suffering, a mission which seemingly led nowhere—

only to the cross. Jesus the missionary met opposition and betrayal with un-changing goodness and gentleness, rooted in his utter reliance and unshakable trust in his Father. Today, in her mission to Asia, the Church will not come in power and wealth. The Church on mission will have to do mission in relative poverty. The Philippine Church, being a Church for the poor, will have "to glory in weakness" and simplicity, so that the real power of God may be revealed. The Filipino missionary will no have great prestige or cultural superiority. He/she must draw instead on the resources, which God alone can give: faith, hope and love, the resources of the Spirit, the virtues and gifts of "the Christ-like God." But such was the mission of Jesus. Let this be a special mark of the Philippines' missionary endeavor, this likeness to Jesus, poor and lowly of heart.

3. *Some Partners in Mission:* Mission, in poverty and humility, following the footsteps of Jesus, will draw much of its strength and power from the prayers and sacrifices of those who will be "stay-at-home missionaries." Here we see the missionary task given to contemplatives, to the sick and aged, to children.

Contemplatives must realize that "the new age of mission" is for them also a new challenge to generosity. Following the footsteps of St. Therese of the Child Jesus, a contemplative, who is declared Patroness of the Missions, they are called to accompany the many missionary activities carried out by those who will "go forth" on missionary journeys and undertake missionary labors. They must renew their faith that their prayer and sacrifices can, in the communion of saints and by the power of the Spirit, be of great support to those who are proclaiming the name and gospel of Jesus to "other peoples."

The sick, who offer their illness and suffering for the Church's missionaries, have a privileged part in missionary endeavor. They are, as the Holy Father has often said, "the strong ones": their self-offering and sacrifices generate much strength from "the power of Jesus' resurrection" for those who toil in the Lord's harvest.

Similarly, children—specially those in our Catholic schools—can be taught again to offer prayers and sacrifices for their brothers and sisters in the mis-sions.The awakening of missionary consciousness and zeal among young people, once so fruitfully done in years gone by, can be renewed. Parents should incul-cate in their children a mission-awareness by giving them information about the missions, by teaching them to pray for the missions and by giving them the example of giving financial support to missionaries. In this way missionary consciousness may come alive again in Christian families and in Christian schools, for otherwise, how can the baptized learn that "every Christian is a missionary"?

4. *Overseas Migrant Filipinos*: We are also to remember that PCP-II stressed "the missionary potential of Filipino migrant workers abroad" (108). It noted that "the wave after wave of Filipinos [who] have sought work in other countries" have produced witnesses "through their religiosity and piety wherever this is possible for them." However, to be effective missionaries these overseas migrant workers should be first evangelized themselves.

5. *Inculturation:* Our own missionary work must foster authentic inculturation within the cultures of Asian peoples to whom Jesus and his Gospel are to be proclaimed; we do not want to repeat the imposition of alien cultural forms in worship, lifestyle and ministry, as was so often done in the past. Creative inculturation in our own communities will instill *attitudes of that catholicity* of the Church, which is the source and end term of missionary inculturation. Thus we hope that Filipino missionary endeavor will bring forth a genuine flowering of inculturated communities, alive to both past and present culture, but also attuned to the changing cultures of our modern and post-modern world. True inculturation, our Asian theologians have repeatedly taught, is really the building up of an authentically local Church for its own time.

6. *Interreligious Dialogue:* Mission in Asia will call for new consciousness and knowledge regarding other religious traditions here in this continent in which almost all the great religions of humanity have been born. One of the "new things" of mission in Asia will be the demand for a deepened understanding of other religious communities (specially the Islamic), their religiosity and their theologies. Attitudes of genuine respect and reverence for others' beliefs and spiritualities must precede and accompany all interreligious dialogue and all mission. The Church's authentic teaching on the relation of Jesus Christ and of the Church herself, to other religions and their traditions as well as a personal experience of living with people of other religions must become, at least in some measure, part of the Christian formation of Asian and Filipino Catholics in the years to come.

7. *Blessed Pedro Calungsod:* We cannot end these reflections without speaking of the great gift given to our people on March 5 of this year: the beatification of Pedro Calungsod, the young—17-year-old—martyr from the Cebu archdiocese. Calungsod gave his life as a missioner of the Gospel in Guam on 2 April 1672. We believe it was a special favor of Divine Providence that the

beatification of such a young person who died a martyr's death several hundred years ago, should take place at the beginning of this Jubilee Year, as the Third Millennium begins—the millennium the Pope has called the "Asian millennium," when Jesus Christ must be proclaimed to Asia. Modern missionaries must be aware that mission work is as difficult and dangerous today as in the past. Like Pedro Calungsod, San Lorenzo Ruiz, the first Filipino Saint, suffered martyrdom for the Faith. Most recently, Fr. Rhoel Gallardo, a missionary in our country, gave up his life for the Faith. Like these three valiant Filipinos, all our missionaries must be ready to endure many trials and hardships including martyrdom for the sake of Christ.

CONCLUSION

We have written this pastoral letter as we prepare for the National Mission Congress. This congress will be our united response, as the People of God in the Philippines, to the great challenge of *Ecclesia in Asia:* we want to begin the millennium by pledging that our local Churches will be truly missionary in spirit and in action, that we will try to realize, every one of us, our call to be missionaries, in our own land, and in our great Asian continent. *We want to promise the Lord, that we as Christian Filipinos will renew our efforts to "tell the world of His love."* We invite above all our beloved young people, to whom Our Lord today turns in a special way, to pledge themselves and their lives to give a living and shining witness to Jesus and His Gospel of truth and love.

We end by invoking Mary, the Mother of the Lord, to accompany us each day as we pray and prepare for the Mission Congress. We, the *pueblo amante de Maria*, do this with immense confidence and hope. As Mary was, in our history, truly and indisputably the Morning Star of our own evangelization, so we know she will go before us, as the Star of the Dawn of the new springtime of the Faith in our continent, and in the whole world itself. To her we pray for all the people of our land, and all the peoples of Asia: "Show unto us the blessed fruit of thy womb, Jesus. *O clement, O loving, O sweet Virgin Mary!"*

For the Catholic Bishops' Conference of the Philippines.

+ORLANDO B. QUEVEDO, OMI
Archbishop of Cotabato
President, CBCP
5 July 2000

Part Seven

ADDITIONAL

RESOURCES

Appendix A

Contribution of the Federation of Asian Bishops' Conferences (FABC) to the Evangelizing Mission of the Church in Asia

Edward F. Malone, MM

Introduction. When Cardinal Vidal wrote me to inform me that the University of San Carlos proposed to confer on me this honorary doctorate, I was taken by surprise. When I mentioned this honor in a phone call to one of my sisters, she exclaimed, "Why?" And, that is indeed the question! But then we all know it is not a personal accolade, so much as a recognition of the pivotal importance of the role that FABC has played through the past thirty years, and continues to play in the growth and enlivenment of the mission of our Church in this part of Asia.

The Church has already acknowledged this missionary influence in the deliberations of the Special Assembly for Asia of the Synod of Bishops, and in the magisterial document of the Holy Father, *Ecclesia in Asia* (The Church in Asia). The continuing progress of our Asian Church also seems in these last two years to have caught the interest of the Church overseas, especially in Africa, Europe and the Western Hemisphere. One little sign is the increasing number of requests for thesis assistance which come into our offices, for researching the beginnings and the present dynamic interaction of FABC's membership. So much documentation is requested that this requires extended research into the files. Fortunately, all of our documentation is now available on the website of the FABC Office of Social Communication in Manila and the website of UCAN News Service in Hong Kong.

So I see today as also a recognition of the collective mass of work that so many dedicated staff members of our seven Offices spread out in several countries have accomplished during these thirty years. Allow me simply to say: they have served, without salaries, and with personal sacrifice, and often with personal hardship.

FABC Contribution. On this happy moment permit me to share some reflections, for someone has appropriately described FABC as "a reflection body of the Asian Church."

First, what is FABC? It is a transnational structure that brings together the fourteen bishops' conferences of East, South and Southeast Asia, consisting of seventeen countries, along with ten ecclesiastical constituencies not yet conferences—twenty-seven countries in all. FABC provides a forum for the exchange of ideas and experiences on "how to be Church" in the modern context and in this part of Asia. It is a totally voluntary organization in membership and in reception—or not—by the bishops' conference or by the individual bishop of any resolutions made by the membership. I wish to emphasize this voluntary character of membership and reception, because often in its wider meetings, this or that resolution would be made: "FABC should do this or that, build this or that, direct this or that," and so forth. The final reply must be that: FABC stands "alongside" the bishops' conferences and the bishops, not "over" them or "in place of them." FABC will help, encourage participation, in short, "be there" when requested, but does not replace the episcopal conference or the bishops.

FABC dates its origin from the visit of Pope Paul VI to Manila in November 1970, when about 180 Asian bishops gathered together for the first time in history. With this vantage point of thirty years (1970-2000) we are able to trace the main lines of the Holy Spirit's action among us of Asia through the FABC. I shall highlight only seven points of mutual discovery, and ever so briefly.

A. Comprehensive Framework for Evangelization. From its inception the FABC zealously sought out how to live and to proclaim the Gospel of Jesus in the new circumstances of our Asian context. In the very first Plenary Assembly in Taipei in 1974, its final statement, entitled *Evangelization in Modern Day Asia* proposed a framework for evangelization. It included elements such as the Proclamation of the Gospel, the Local Church, Dialogue with the

Religions of Asia, Dialogue with the Poor, and especially with the Cultures, Missionary Formation, and the Messengers of the Gospel. One phrase from this FABC Assembly has become a kind of pastoral axiom: a call for a "triple dialogue: with Asia's peoples, their cultures and religions." This summary has stayed with our Church in Asia through these three decades, sustaining a vision which encompasses every part of our evangelical work.

B. Asian Theological Reflection. The FABC Office of Theological Concerns (now also with an ecumenical thrust!) has had a three-fold goal: to foster theological thought on issues that are of special concern for our Asian Churches; to assist the FABC membership in conceptualizing and making policies for missionary and pastoral action; and, to promote the development of a theology that is contemporary and relevant to our Asian countries and to the wider Church as well. Six significant documents have emerged from this community of theologians: on interreligious dialogue (1987), the local Church (1990), political involvement (1992), a theology of harmony (1995), the working of the Holy Spirit in Asia (1997), and Methodology: Towards an Asian Christian Theology (2000).

C. Pastoral Methodology and Pastoral Priorities. Our Church in Asia seeks to proclaim the Gospel in Asia, and for this task FABC has also developed through its Office of Laity a unique approach, simply called "the Asian Integrated Pastoral Approach," or AsIPA. It employs what is called the "pastoral cycle," with four dimensions. It begins with exposure-immersion into daily realities: one enters a *dialogue of life*. The second stage is *social analysis*, which includes the religious-cultural dimension. The third stage, the *contemplative dimension*, seeks to discover God's presence and activity in the Asian context. The final stage is *pastoral planning* which seeks results in actual, realizable plans. In addition, the FABC VI Assembly identified as crucial and central five major pastoral areas of discipleship: the Asian family, women and the girl-child, the youth, ecology, and the displaced (political and ecological refugees and migrant workers).

D. Church Community and Motivation for Mission. The FABC VI calls for genuine inculturated and indigenous local Church communities, which alone can be agents for the self-realization of the Church. They are the "acting subject of Mission." Because these communities incarnate "a new way of being Church," they are committed to becoming a "community of communities" (another working axiom!). They have clear doctrinal motives for engaging in the mission of the Church: gratitude, the mandate of Christ, faith, baptism, leaven.

E. Programs for Bishops in Effective Pastoral Leadership. Probably the two most effective programs of leadership training are the BIRA series (the Bishops' Institute for Interreligious Dialogue) which assists bishops in interreligious dialogue through exposure and reflection; and the "Effective Leadership for Bishops" courses, about 20 of them, which have brought together for sharing and training about 325 of our bishops in a "dramatic" participation for their ministry as bishops for the "little flocks" of Asia.

F. Sharing the Asian Church with Universal Church. Through its published documentation FABC has also shared its experience, ideas, insights and theology of our Asian local Churches with the Universal Church. One important—and startling—event took place during the Synod on Evangelization when one of the Synodal secretaries, the late Father Amalorpavadass, was able to bring many elements of what we now consider our Asian theological and pastoral heritage into the Synodal Hall. And perhaps, we can detect these strains of a new vision, in what later became Pope Paul VI's *Evangelii Nuntiandi.*

G. Seventh FABC Plenary Assembly. Allow me also to refer you to the documentation of the recent Seventh FABC Plenary Assembly held in January of this Holy Year [2000], in Samphran, Thailand, and to its Final Statement, a superb summary in a few pages of the apostolic movement of our Local Churches of Asia in the past and for the future, which appears as *FABC Paper No. 93,* to which I refer you. Here we have a vision and a beckoning for the future of our beloved Church in Asia and of ourselves—faithful servants that we hope to be of the Lord Jesus.

Finally, I wish to thank you for giving me this opportunity to highlight how the FABC is really a "missionary assembly" of Asian Bishops, and of the Christian communities gathered with them. I wish to thank all those in this important assembly who through the years shared themselves to make FABC work.

Special Memories. Our Church in Asia owes so much to the Philippine Church. Here is the cradle where the FABC was born and nourished through its 30 years of life.

The other night as I was falling to sleep and at the same time thinking what I could—and should—say here, some of my favorite moments in the Philippines came to memory. These I recall vividly; there are others too:

>>>   of sitting with Cardinal Santos in 1973 when as a small group we discussed the future of Radio Veritas, and his fantastic memory for details.

>>>   of another Cardinal, Cardinal Jaime Sin, then still archbishop and new to Manila, addressing the bishops of Asia in Taipei, in 1974, in the first Plenary Assembly, standing there in his leather jacket pulled around him because it was cold, and promising the bishops that, if the bishops wanted it, he would revitalize Radio Veritas. The bishops voted that they wanted it; and the Cardinal said: "If I don't, you can have my head." He still has his head, you see.

>>>   and Bishop Julio Labayen, with his small group, bringing the social message of the Church first to the priests through PISA and then to the bishops through BISA, from a little desk in Manila, and helping FABC to get formed to see the every need of our poor in Asia.

>>>   and especially Father Catalino Arévalo and Archbishop Gaudencio Rosales, who in assemblies and publications brought to us the vision of a renewed Church at the heart of the world! I read today some of our early statements, and am always deeply moved. For myself, I call them a liturgy of "the workings of the Triune God."

>>>   and of many others: especially for this meeting and of Archbishop Mariano Gaviola and Archbishop Oscar Cruz, FABC secretaries general, with whom I served and with whom I shared a deep friendship.

Conclusion. I could go on and on—ask my students of years ago! But finally, what else does FABC mean to our "Church in Asia." After the Roman Special Assembly for Asia of the Synod of Bishops, one of our Asian bishops told me that a Roman Cardinal confided to him: "It is obvious that you Asian bishops have come prepared; you also know each other—and he paused—and you like each other too!" Now that is real success.

So FABC is all these things I said before, and more. Years ago I wrote my doctoral thesis on the doctrinal meaning of apostolic zeal. In those days there was not much written on it. I really suffered in doing my research. I went to the famous Father Garrigou-Lagrange, because I could not find sources; he asked me why I had picked the topic, and then helped me.

After many months of research and thinking I came to the startling conclusion (for then) that apostolic zeal is only the intense, devoted friendship with Christ and Jesus with us. I think this is also something that FABC has discovered and shared with the Church in Asia: friendship, community, participation, involvement with the Lord and each other. May this always be!

Thank you for inviting me to be present at this Mission Congress. God bless you all. *Daghang salamat. Adios.*

[Editor's Note: This address was given at the Conferment Rites held at the University of San Carlos Cultural Center on September 30, 2000; Father Edward F. Malone, MM and Archbishop Charles A. Schleck, CSC, DD, were awarded doctorates *honoris causa* for their unique contributions to mission.]

ART EXPRESSES CHURCH'S MISSION

James H. Kroeger, MM

"The Church needs art in order to communicate the message entrusted to her by Christ"—words of Pope John Paul II in his 1999 *Letter to Artists*. "Art has the unique capacity to take one or other facet of the message and translate it into colors, shapes, and sounds which nourish the intuition of those who look or listen.... The Church has need especially of those who can do this on the literary and figurative level, using the endless possibilities of images and their symbolic force" (12).

This vision of art at the service of the Gospel and mission lies behind the effort to design an attractive book for the National Mission Congress in Cebu. The result is *Tell the World...* an integrated program of mission awareness and catechesis. The organizers of the Mission Congress believed that if attractive and practical materials were readily available, probably many more persons in parishes, schools, Christian communities, and reflection groups would be drawn to understand and participate in the task of mission, the central and holiest work of the Church.

Tell the World... with its unique cover visually portrays dynamic people; it captures the "Church-in-Mission." This brief essay is a reflection on the insightful and profound meaning expressed in the painting. Father Benny Justiniano, a diocesan priest from Bulacan, has done the Church and her mission a great service through his expressive, professional art.

Who forms this missionary Church—especially in the context of the Philippines? Who is the pilgrim Church which is to be "missionary by her very nature" (AG 2)? How are we to be a "community-in-mission" in the Asian world of today? Permit some reflections—inspired by the dynamic back cover painting of *Tell the World...*. [*Note:* paragraph numbers correspond to the numbers on the painting itself].

"Church–in–Mission"

(1) Jesus is the first missionary of his heavenly Father. God who is love "sent his only Son into the world so that we can have life through him" (I John 4:9). Jesus called his followers and formed the Church, a community-of-disciples-in-mission. In giving the gift of the Holy Spirit to his disciples, Jesus said, "As the Father sent me, so am I sending you" (John 20:21). Mission originates in the bosom of the Trinity and is revealed through Jesus and the Holy Spirit in the heart of the Church.

(2) The Blessed Virgin Mary, Mother of the Lord, is the Morning Star of Evangelization. Mary was the first to hear the Word of God, receive it joyfully in her heart, and bring it to the waiting world. The Church constantly looks to Mary as a model and guide in leading people to Jesus Christ. As Mary prayerfully waited with the disciples in the upper room on that first Pentecost, she now accompanies the Church-in-mission. She is Queen of the Apostles and "Mother of Asia" (*Ecclesia in Asia* 51).

(3) Saint Therese of the Child Jesus (1873-97) together with Francis Xavier were declared "patrons of all mission" in 1927. Therese's famous title "The Little Flower" derives from her image of herself as only one among millions of little flowers on the hillside, each giving its all in joy and praise to God. From the seclusion of her Carmelite monastery in Lisieux, France, she profoundly contributed to the Church's mission—by prayer, suffering, and virtue. She saw her vocation to be love in the heart of Mother Church. Thousands of Filipinos reverenced her relics during her Philippine visit in the Jubilee Year 2000.

(4) Saint Francis Xavier (1506-52) was a student at the University of Paris when he met Ignatius of Loyola. At age 34 he left Europe for Asia where he labored in India, Malaysia, Indonesia, and Japan; he never again returned to Europe. He was indefatigable in his zeal to serve mission effectively. When Xavier realized that most Asians regarded China as the cultural capital of the world, he shifted his attention and sought to enter China. After twelve years of zealous, active mission, but already a legend in both Europe and Asia, the forty-six-year-old Jesuit died of a fever while on his way to China.

(5) Saint Lorenzo Ruiz was born around the beginning of the seventeenth century; he served the Dominican Fathers as a clerk (*escribano*) in the parish of Binondo, Manila. Lorenzo joined the Dominicans on a missionary journey to Japan, where they were arrested and imprisoned. During the trial Lorenzo professed his faith: "I am a Christian and I will remain so until the hour of my

death.... I would rather die a thousand deaths than renounce my faith." Lorenzo and his companions were tried and sentenced to death. Beatified in 1981 by Pope John Paul II in Manila and canonized in 1987 in Rome, Lorenzo's feastday is celebrated on September 28.

(6) Blessed Pedro Calungsod was a teenage lay Catholic Christian from the Visayas who served the Jesuit Mission in the Marianas as a catechist and mission helper. Pedro was the lone companion of Father Diego Luis de San Vitores, SJ, the Spanish superior of the Marianas mission on the morning of April 2, 1672 when both met martyrdom. They were killed for being Christians, for catechizing the Mariana natives, and for administering the Sacrament of Baptism. Father San Vitores was beatified on October 6, 1985, while Pedro Calungsod was beatified during the Jubilee Year on March 5, 2000.

(7) Mother Teresa, popularly known during her lifetime as the living saint, was born in Albania in 1911. After spending several years teaching in her order's Catholic schools in India, she felt the call from God to go out into the streets and care for the most desperate people. For them she organized orphanages, houses for the elderly and dying, hospitals and care facilities. She founded a new religious congregation, the Missionaries of Charity, with the vow to give their life for the poorest of the poor. In 1979 she was awarded the Nobel Peace Prize. Asked how she loved people whom others regarded as human debris, she replied: "My secret is quite simple. I pray." Mother Teresa, a woman of deep faith, is a true missionary for our times.

(8) Pope John Paul II was born of a modest family in Poland on May 18, 1920. He desired to become a priest, but was forced to study secretly since the Germans had closed the Krakow seminary. He was elected pope in 1978 at the age of 58, the first non-Italian pope in 500 years. In 1981 he was shot and seriously wounded by Mehemet Ali Agca, whom he visited in prison and forgave. In 1982 he pilgrimaged to Fatima to present a bullet and thank the Virgin for deliverance from assassination; his motto *Totus Tuus* (I am totally yours) emphasizes his personal consecration to the Virgin Mary. He has become known as the "pilgrim pope"; in his mission encyclical *Redemptoris Missio*, he wrote: "From the beginning of my Pontificate I have chosen to travel to the ends of the earth in order to show this missionary concern" (1).

(9) Communities of indigenous persons or *lumads* are found in most Asian countries; the Philippines has a rich diversity of native peoples and some have

become members of the Church. Yet, these communities often experience discrimination and prejudice in the attitudes of mainstream citizens. The Church seeks to promote the protection of their lands and domains, the recognition of their cultural integrity, and the respect of their unique social-political processes. The Church in the Philippines strives to address their community needs through the CBCP Commission on Indigenous Peoples.

(**10**) Professional and Business People constitute an important sector of any local church. As laity active in "public life," that is, in the many different economic, social, legislative, administrative and cultural areas, their mission is to promote the common good of all citizens. Since Filipino Catholic laity constitute the great majority in this nation, they hold "primary responsibility for building a just Philippine society" (CFC, 1193).

(**11**) Students and Young People are both a gift and a challenge within the Church. Already in 1987 it was recognized that half of the world's population was below 25 years old; a high percentage of youth are concentrated in developing countries—like the Philippines. Youth are not to be viewed as the object of the Church's pastoral care; they are "agents and co-workers in the Church's mission in her various apostolic works of love and service" (*Ecclesia in Asia* 47). The mission potential of youth is a great treasure; is it often a hidden or undiscovered resource?

(**12**) Beggars, street urchins, abused children—they are frequently "society's victims"; yet, they are all God's little ones. Where do they run for love and care, for food and shelter? Where can they find a safe haven to learn to put their lives together and become responsible, self-reliant adults? Can the Church put more of her resources and personnel at the disposal of this growing sector of society? What are the unjust societal structures that create such inhuman situations? The list of questions—genuine mission questions—seems endless.

(**13**) Priests and deacons, all ordained ministers, are meant to serve the Christian community and all those in need. The outpouring of the Spirit in the sacrament of orders configures the recipient to Christ. Thus, the priest's life and mission are to be marked by the virtue of "pastoral charity." This demands being conformed to Christ—humble servant, good shepherd, gentle leader, compassionate minister. Priestly "configuration to Christ" does not imply privilege; it demands self-giving and service in the Church's evangelizing mission.

(**14**) Mother-nun-teacher-madre, they are the world's special care-givers,

God's compassion in person. They daily incarnate love as they teach, cook, wash, console, educate, embrace, smile. The world's women are missionaries in the small, hidden, often insignificant, spaces of life. What a sublime vocation! The awakening of Church-people to the dignity and rights of women is one of the most significant signs of the times—it must receive continued attention in the Church's mission.

(15-16) Children, noted for their receptivity, trusting attitude, and ready smile, have something to teach the Church about mission. "Unless you change and become like little children, you will never enter the kingdom of heaven" (Matthew 18:3). "Let the little children come to me, and do not stop them; for it is to such as these that the kingdom of God belongs" (Luke 18:16). Recall the vision of spirituality of Saint Therese of Lisieux, the patroness of mission; her insight focuses on "the Little Way," the way of spiritual childhood.

(17) The farmer and common laborer (they are often fathers of families) equally share in the mission of the Church. A man of integrity, faith and simple goodness, a responsible parent, dedicated breadwinner, loving husband, selfless father—these are the qualities of the man whose very life is a model of Christian witness. Social status, academic degrees, annual income or size of home are not criteria of a Christian life-style. Mission is for all.

(18) Mahatma Gandhi, Asia's great apostle of non-violent social transformation, has much to teach Christians about mission. "The teaching of the Sermon [on the Mount] was meant for each and every one of us.... I can say that a life of service and uttermost simplicity is the best preaching.... I have a definite feeling that if you want us to feel the aroma of Christianity, you must copy the rose.... A rose does not need to preach. It simply spreads its fragrance. The fragrance is its own sermon."

Concluding Reflection. Christian mission in its diversity, complexity, beauty and richness can be read on people's faces. Each person reveals a new dimension of what it means to be a part of an evangelizing community, a member of the missionary church. Each of the eighteen personages in Father Benny Justiniano's artistic portrayal of the "Church-in-Mission" reveals another facet of evangelization.

And yet, these are not eighteen separate, isolated individuals. All are united into the one Church of Christ: united with the Lord Jesus, his mother Mary, the saints in glory—Therese, Xavier, Lorenzo, Pedro; united with our brothers and sisters who may be church leaders, businessmen and farmers, professionals and students; united by our common faith and baptism in the one Spirit; united in bonds of fraternal love and charity, ready to be in mission as servants of God's coming kingdom, ready to **Tell the World,** yes, to announce to everyone "the breadth and the length, the height and the depth ... of the love of God" (Ephesians 3:18-19).

Tell the World... is unique among books—you CAN recognize it by its cover. You are invited to follow Christ, Mary, Xavier and Therese, Calungsod and Ruiz into the heart of this book—into the heart of mission.